'Alpha continues to be one of the most anointed ministries of our times. Optimizing the full redemptive potential of Alpha in local churches is something Tricia Neill knows better than anyone in the world. This book will support the work of the local church.'

Bill Hybels, Senior Pastor, Willow Creek Community Church, Chicago

'Tricia Neill is one of the most effective managers that I have come across. Her focus on the practical and actionable is intense, and results in a lot more getting done than is the norm. I'd highly recommend any manager to read this ... tremendously helpful book.'

Dr Alistair M. Hanna, Former Director, McKinsey and Company

'HTB and Alpha are both phenomenally successful organisations, and this book gives you an insider's view of the principles that led to their growth. Tricia Neill shares these principles without any trace of pride, and with a simplicity and honesty

that is endearing. I recommend this book to those who want tried and tested principles to help their churches grow.'

Pastor Agu Irukwu, Senior Pastor,
Jesus House, London

'Drawing on her years of experience in both the corporate world and a thriving church community, Tricia Neill has given us a template for turning vision into action. Like Alpha, it too will prove to be a valuable tool for those desiring to lead their churches into the future.'

Phil Jeansonne, Senior Pastor,
The Vineyard Church, New Orleans

'*From Vision to Action* is more than simply another "how-to" church growth book. It is a consultation with one of the clearest and most encouraging strategic thinkers in the Christian movement today.'

Revd Dr Tory Baucum, Rector,
Truro Church, Virginia

'This is a fast-moving and clearly written book that every church leader should read. Tricia demonstrates how she has helped take a vision and played a huge part in building something that will last.'

Mark Bailey, Lead Pastor, Trinity Cheltenham & New Wine Leadership Team

'*From Vision to Action* is easy to read, practical, and realistic, and shows an understanding based on hands-on experience of how to move a church forward into God's vision, and how to keep it there.'

Charles Whitehead, Former President, International Catholic Charismatic Renewal Services

'Tricia Neill is wonderfully practical in all she sets her mind to, and not least the details of making church happen in practice. This is a treasure chest of godly insights that I have found profoundly helpful – not just as I read it, but also as I put it into practice.'

Revd Ric Thorpe, Rector, St Paul's Church Shadwell, London

'Tricia Neill is the real thing. She has a spectacular spiritual gift of administration. My experience has been that she subdues chaos and releases life. This book shows how the body of Christ struggles to flourish without proper administration. The wisdom distilled here in generous and easy to read fashion will strengthen and liberate the church to be more truly itself.'

**Revd Simon Downham, Vicar,
St Paul's Hammersmith, London**

'This book is a recipe for success in the local church. Use it and you experience the change.'

**Graeme Paris, Executive Director,
Willow Creek UK & Ireland**

'This vitally important publication can lead Christian groups and churches from a hand to mouth existence to one of purpose and passion.'

**Gerald Coates, Founder of Pioneer,
Speaker, Author, Broadcaster**

'*From Vision to Action* draws out the real workings and "goings-on" behind the scenes, and allows other churches to learn from what God has taught HTB over the last few years.'

**Revd Frog and Amy Orr-Ewing,
Latimer Minster, Beaconsfield, London**

'HTB is a church with a passionate concern for God's glory, a genuine concern for the church at large, a faithfulness to prayer, and a spirit of humility with a childlike dependence on the work of the Spirit and his grace. With these values in place, it is not a wonder that leadership and management principles work so effectively. There is something special happening here. It needs to be reflected on for the benefit of others. I am glad *From Vision to Action* does that.'

Revd Terry Wong, St James' Church, Singapore

'Tricia Neill has written a superb book that should give a huge amount of help to any harried church minister or overwhelmed church administrator. I wish I had had such a book many years ago, to help me through the daunting task of moving a church forward.'

Malcolm Round, Rector, St Mungo's Balerno

'This book is filled with nuggets of practical wisdom for local churches about how to turn God-given vision into reality. Tricia shares the effective strategies and managements that have enabled the life-changing ministries of Alpha and HTB to "take off" all over the world.'

Revd Lyndon Bowring,
Executive Chairman, Care

'Effective ministry should be the goal of every Christian and their church. Drawing upon her experience at HTB, Tricia Neill contributes valuable insights to encourage this.'

Dr Raymond Muller, National Director,
Alpha New Zealand, Former Archdeacon

'This will become a core point of reference for the leadership of our church.'

Revd John Valentine, Rector,
St George's Holborn, London

FROM VISION TO ACTION

PRACTICAL STEPS FOR CHURCH GROWTH

TRICIA NEILL

First published 2006
Reprinted 2009
Reprinted 2011
This new edition 2013

ISBN: 978 1 905887 98 9 (Print)
978 1 907950 69 8 (epub)
978 1 907950 70 4 (Kindle)
978 1 907950 77 3 (PDF)

Published by Alpha International
HTB Brompton Road
London
SW7 1JA
Email: publications@alpha.org
Website: alpha.org
Printed and bound in Great Britain by Clays Ltd, St Ives PLC

CONTENTS

FOREWORD

For all of us who have been involved with Holy Trinity Brompton (HTB), Tricia Neill is an institution. Her professionalism, clear-sightedness and common sense pervade every aspect of the church's life.

For many years we had a dream that the way we ran things in Christian circles would rival the best of what we saw elsewhere. But we did not know how to do it. Now we do. You find a Tricia – and stand back!

She came to us, of course, with considerable experience of top-class management, latterly with Rupert Murdoch's News International group, where she ran its exhibition and conference division.

I remember well her arrival on our staff in 1994, soon after completing Alpha at the church. Within a very short time, meetings were being organised – each with a clear purpose and direction. Notes were being made of decisions that were then acted upon.

Gradually Tricia built up a culture of professionalism across the whole staff, which I was privileged simply to watch and wonder at.

Amid all this activity, Tricia's grace, kindness and tact has been at the centre of it all. Her sheer sensitivity to those around her is abundant. I cannot think of anybody who has felt anything other than built up by what she has to say – even difficult things.

Those of us who have worked at Holy Trinity Brompton have been convinced that – 'Every church needs a Tricia.' But I'm afraid HTB hope to hang on to her for some time yet!

In the meantime, with the help of this revised edition of the book, we can continue to share her wisdom and expertise.

Sandy Millar
Assistant Bishop, Diocese of
St Edmundsbury and Ipswich,
Vicar of HTB 1985–2005

INTRODUCTION

This book is primarily concerned with the ins and outs of church management. It is for leaders of churches of all sizes who are looking for effective ways to carry out whatever vision God has given them – leaders of churches who want to 'move their church forward'.

I have been asked time and time again how we have worked through growth here at HTB and this book helps to address these questions.

A part of the HTB vision is to share what we have been given by God with other churches. 'Giving it away' is one of our driving philosophies. I hope that through this book we are 'giving away' some of the knowledge we have gained and some of the lessons we have learned along the way. It represents a collection of tried-and-tested methods that we have been using and improving upon for more than nineteen years.

It has been an enormous privilege to be involved in the growth of Alpha. I never fail to be excited by the stories of lives changing and churches growing the world over as a result. Here at HTB, we experienced this growth when Alpha became central to all that we did. As new people joined our church, we addressed the way we ran things.

Sandy Millar, former vicar of HTB, asked me early on in my time here: 'Why shouldn't the church work more professionally and better than any good secular organisation?' When training churches to run Alpha, we encourage them to treat their guests better than any secular course would treat them. Sandy was instrumental in setting this high standard for the running of the church as well.

> 'WHY SHOULDN'T THE CHURCH WORK MORE PROFESSIONALLY AND BETTER THAN ANY GOOD SECULAR ORGANISATION?'
>
> – Sandy Millar

Nicky Gumbel – pioneer of Alpha and now vicar of HTB – has remarked that there are three types of people: those who make things happen; those who watch things happen and those who haven't a clue what's happening. While I suspect many of us would like to be in the first category, I think we all too often fall into the last.

One of the first types who make things happen is Ric Thorpe, a former curate at HTB and now rector of St Paul's Church, Shadwell, in the East End of London. Ric has been a huge encourager of this book from the start, but he pointed out to me some time after the printing of the first edition that perhaps people needed help with establishing a vision.

It was an excellent point. When I arrived, Sandy and Nicky had been very clear about the vision. There was no shortage of vision with them! They just needed help in realising their dreams.

Ric pointed out that, when the time came for him to plant his church into the East End (he took a group of fifty people from HTB), he tossed and turned as he tried to pin down exactly what *his* vision was. And without a clear vision upon which to set to work, this book was not going to be of much help.

It is not as if Ric was lacking in drive. On the contrary, he was full of vigour and resolve. His marketing background and his time at Sandy Millar's side as a senior member of his lay staff ensured that he was full of ability.

So how did he approach this task of formulating a vision? He has written his fascinating and helpful account of how to do this, and I have included it as an invaluable supplementary chapter at the end of this new edition.

I appreciate that identifying a vision can be a challenge but Ric shows that, by using a few simple processes beginning with what he calls a 'spark', this can be achieved.

Let me say that this book isn't intended to presume that we at HTB know it all – certainly not – we have learned many lessons over the years, particularly from the experience of other churches.

I also recognise that, for many, our situation at HTB – even in 1994 when we had so few staff – may not seem relevant. I know that many churches have no paid staff at all. Nevertheless, we use many of the same approaches for working with both volunteers and staff and set the same standards. In addition, many people who have worked at HTB have found that the techniques they have learned have proved to be very useful when they subsequently moved on to churches of different sizes. As I have developed this book, people involved with churches, small, medium and large, have reviewed it. I have been most grateful for their enthusiasm and input.

I hope that you will find that you can relate to some of what follows and apply it to your own churches to enable you to get where you want to be.

Finally, it is important to state early on that everything we try to do at HTB is undergirded with prayer. We know that without prayer the approaches discussed here would not amount to much.

It has been a great privilege to work with Sandy Millar and Nicky Gumbel and I am hugely grateful for the opportunities they have given me, which form the basis of this book.

I would like to thank Jamie McLean and Jo Rice for the fun of working with them and for their assistance in writing this, and also Ric Thorpe, Emma Barnes and Thommy Tillotson for their invaluable help in updating the second edition. I have loved working with you on this. I am also grateful to Mark Elsdon-Dew, Alpha International staff and all those who have read the manuscript, for their wisdom and input.

We hope you will find the ideas helpful and wish you every success in moving your God-given vision forward.

Tricia Neill

TRICIA'S STORY

I was brought up in Northumberland, in the UK. I had a very happy childhood and as a family we attended the local Presbyterian church.

All I ever wanted to do was teach, so as soon as I left school I went off to train as a teacher. I was terribly excited about leaving home, and from that moment I never went to church again. I just didn't see the relevance of Christianity for my life.

In my third year of teaching at a primary school in Newcastle, I saw a job advertised in The Sunday Times. Shell, the oil company, had schools for children of their workforce all around the world – and they wanted teachers. I applied, and after about six months of interviewing I was offered a job in the Sultanate of Oman.

I'd never heard of Oman but in 1978 I went to live there. I knew within two hours of my arrival that I completely loved it. I loved the country, I loved the school, I loved the children, I loved the life. It was all so new and very exciting.

I stayed in the Middle East for seven years. Within a year, I was made deputy headmistress of the school. I enjoyed every moment of my job and the lifestyle it afforded – boats, helicopters, parties, drinking and a whirling social life.

Eventually my contract ran out with Shell and I had to leave. I came back to London in about 1985 and decided that I didn't want to teach any more. I was keen to try something new.

Within a week of being in London, a friend phoned me up and said, 'Trish, our company is desperate for help. Can you just come in and help us for a week or two?' The company was called World Trade Promotions, and the job was helping to market and organise exhibitions right across the globe.

Towards the end of my first week there, the managing director asked me to stay on the staff. The exhibitions were in Hong Kong, Chicago, Brussels and other major cities. All of them were abroad and I loved travelling, so I said yes. It was a tremendous training ground for me.

Five years later, in 1990, I was approached by News International, owned by Rupert Murdoch, to set up an exhibition company for them. They asked me to help spearhead a new company based in London, which would put on consumer exhibitions marketed through their British newspapers (which at the time included The Sun, News of the World, The Times, The Sunday Times and Today).

I was really excited about it because it was a new company and I love starting up new things. We began recruiting lots of people, and soon we were organising exhibitions all over the UK. I was involved in quite a fast-paced executive lifestyle by then. I worked hard and I played hard too. I did find London a lonely place to live and, compared to my time in the Middle East, I found making friends more difficult in a big city. I always felt there could be more to life than I was experiencing.

One of the highlights of my week after moving to London was that I joined a tennis club in Wimbledon (the Wimbledon Club, opposite the All England Club), and used to play every Saturday. I made many good friends there. Two of the girls went to church; they were the first Christians I had met since I left home, and one day they invited me to an Alpha supper party at their church.

They told me there would be lots of nice people and that it would be great fun. I liked them so I thought I'd try it. I'm usually game for something new.

When I went to the Alpha supper – at a church I didn't know at the time called HTB – I didn't really enjoy it. The food and the company were good but the after-dinner talk by a speaker called Nicky Gumbel was just too much for me. I didn't like it at all.

When Jean, one of the friends who had invited me, asked how it had gone and whether I might consider going on Alpha, I said, 'Jean, I'm seriously not interested and I'd be grateful if you'd never mention it to me ever again.'

About nine months later I was chatting to a neighbour who lived opposite me. As we were speaking she told me, with tears in her eyes, that her husband had been having an affair with his secretary for some time. She said, 'I don't know how I'm going to get through this. All my friends are very superficial and just party people.' I felt so sad for her and didn't know how to help.

Then I heard myself say to her, 'You ought to go on an Alpha Course. You'll meet some nice people there.' And to my horror I added, 'And if you want I'll come with you and keep you company.'

She said, 'I'd like to go.' And I thought, 'Help! I'm going on Alpha!' So I went on Alpha in January 1993.

When I arrived for the first week of

'YOU OUGHT TO GO ON AN ALPHA COURSE. YOU'LL MEET SOME NICE PEOPLE THERE.' AND TO MY HORROR I ADDED, 'AND IF YOU WANT I'LL COME WITH YOU AND KEEP YOU COMPANY.'

the course I was shocked. Here were all these nice, normal people discussing whether God existed. But what if he did? What difference was it going to make? On the way home I felt so unsettled by it all that I said to my neighbour I had to stop for a whisky – so we pulled in to a pub.

Despite this inauspicious start I gradually found that my attitude began to change. I began to go to Alpha for myself. I wasn't going just to keep my friend company any more, and I was intrigued. I began to join in the group discussion, and soon realised that I was looking forward to it each week.

On the Wednesday morning after the Alpha weekend, I was sitting at my dining room table.

I had started reading the Bible, and had come across the notion of the cost of being a disciple when I thought, 'I want to be a Christian. I would give up everything and anything for that.' So I prayed and told God that I was sorry for all the things I had done wrong in my life and that I wanted a new start.

That morning – it was in February 1993 – I gave my life to Jesus. I was so excited. It was like I was in love for the first time – an extraordinary feeling. My priorities began to change – my lifestyle that had previously been so important no longer seemed to matter.

When Alpha was over I was invited to help on the next course, and the next one. I also joined a prayer group. One day, some months later, I got back to my office at News International and there were three telephone messages on my desk.

One said, 'Please call Nicky Gumbel urgently.'

The next one said, 'Please ring Jeremy' [the former Financial Director of HTB].

And the third said, 'Please ring Judy [a member of HTB's PCC] urgently.'

So I thought, 'Well, something is up.'

I rang Nicky and he very sweetly asked me if I would be prepared to leave my job and come to HTB to work with him. He didn't quite know what my job would be, but could I finish my job today and start on the following Monday. That's typical of Nicky.

I laughed and said, 'I don't think so, Nicky.' And that was it. Or so I thought.

The following Tuesday I went to my little prayer group and they asked, 'How's your week been?' I said, 'You won't believe this ....'

And I roared with laughter and said, 'Nicky Gumbel asked if I would come and work with him at HTB.'

And they said, 'Well, what did you say?'

And I said, 'Well, I said "no" of course.'

And they said, 'Well, don't you think you should pray about it?'

I was completely shocked. As a new Christian I hadn't realised that I could ask for God's help with questions or issues I was facing. So after that I started praying.

That weekend, at a friend's very traditional wedding, I looked around at the lovely group of people attending and was moved by the thought that this occasion might be the only opportunity they had to hear the gospel. I was sitting in the back row, and as I watched all of these people sitting in front of me I just started crying. I suddenly felt an overwhelming desire that everyone there should have the opportunity to do Alpha.

While I was still genuinely struggling with the idea of saying 'yes' to the job, I began to feel I just couldn't say 'no'.

About two weeks before I finally accepted, I was offered the position of Director of News International Exhibitions. It was the post I had wanted – everything I had been working for, with a huge pay increase and so on. But when I was offered it, I just thought, 'So what?'

It didn't mean anything to me. When I finally rang Nicky to accept HTB's offer, I knew I had made the right choice.

On my first day working at HTB, in April 1994, I drove in at about 8:30 am and opened the boot of my car. I got my stuff out. I looked around, and I couldn't find anybody. I could not find a single person. Eventually I came across a man with a hammer in his hand. I said, 'I wonder if you could help me? My name's Tricia and I'm just starting today.' He beamed at that and said, 'Oh! I'm just off to build you an office.'

I was terribly upset because they'd known I was coming for three months. But when I arrived, I had no office, no desk, no phone. I had nothing. I remember feeling very sorry for myself and thinking, 'I've given up so much – and this is what I've come to.'

Later on I remember thinking, 'No other staff member's ever going to have that happen to them when they arrive so long as I am here.'

As I went around to meet the small number of staff, everyone was very helpful and enthusiastic but there was very little structure to what they were doing. There were no job specifications. Nobody knew who was reporting to whom. In a sense they were not making the most of the advantages they had, being what was – even then – one of the biggest and most well-known churches in the UK.

During my first year at HTB, I was working mostly on helping to support the growth of Alpha outside of HTB. Alpha was exploding, and many churches were interested in running it. My time was spent trying to see how we could structure Alpha in the UK and around the world, so churches could be trained to run Alpha wherever they were, as well as obtain Alpha materials in a language and at a cost relevant to them. It was hugely exciting but very hard work! However, we found that after a year all we had done was react to the demand. We had not actually planned the way forward in a structured, systematic way.

I recall saying to Nicky that I had never previously approached my work in this way – merely reacting to circumstances, rather than planning where we were trying to get to. During that first year I used to feel as if I was trapped on a conveyor belt, and while all this was happening I remember being asked if I could manage with only a part-time assistant. My answer was firmly in the negative. The perception at first was that I did not need much help. There was a lack of understanding that the right administrative support could make our ministry so much more effective.

After about three years at HTB, we could see we were attaining the professional standards and structures for Alpha that we desired. Sandy also passionately wanted these things for HTB as the parish church – a natural consequence of Alpha being at the very heart of the church. We set about incorporating the ideas, professionalism and processes of Alpha into the running of HTB itself. At that time Sandy created a leadership team of himself, Nicky and me over both Alpha and HTB, so that we were responsible for all activities in both these areas. Each of the three of us had a clearly defined role – Sandy as the senior church leader responsible for the vision, Nicky as the practitioner, and myself as the implementer. This model worked very well, as there was one person on the team whose job it was to make it all happen.

We definitely reaped positive results from applying business principles in a Christian way, and God has blessed us enormously over these past years. Since 1994, I have had the privilege of seeing

> 'WE DEFINITELY REAPED POSITIVE RESULTS FROM APPLYING BUSINESS PRINCIPLES IN A CHRISTIAN WAY'.

twenty-six new church plants go from HTB, and seeing Alpha run with more than 1,000 people involved. When I arrived there were 200 Alpha Courses; now there are over 66,000 in 169 countries. In fact, over 20 million people have attended Alpha. I have watched the number of pastorate groups grow to more than 100, and seen the expansion of Sunday services to eleven. We now have over 400 people on our staff and have opened 51 Alpha offices around the world, having officially translated Alpha into 112 languages. The rate of growth has been astounding, and, in 2001, the decision was taken to set up Alpha International as a charity, separate from HTB. It was a very, very exciting time. So I have to say that, since that first, bleak, Monday morning, when I first started at HTB, life has certainly been far from dull.

I hope that the steps and principles we have used, which are laid out in the following chapters, will serve to inspire and benefit you and your particular church context.

CASTING THE VISION

ARTICULATE YOUR VISION

Our vision statement at HTB and Alpha International is to play our part in 'the re-evangelisation of the nations and the transformation of society'. You probably already have a sense of what God wants to do through the ministry of your church, or maybe there is simply an inner longing for change as you have seen the impact of Alpha within your parish. The steps we at HTB took to develop our vision have changed over the years, as we ourselves have grown.

SET THE BASELINE

When we first embarked on the systematic process of applying business principles to the running of HTB, we looked at and addressed what we believed

God was calling us to do. We asked ourselves what we thought our future should look like, and what the vision for our church was.

We then looked at our current situation. We examined what we were achieving and what we were not. We noted where we were, and where we wanted to be. We looked at specific areas such as the number of services, the number in the congregation and the profile of the parish. That became the baseline for any comparison we were working towards. For example, in a particular year, we decided we wanted to see ten new pastorates and twenty new volunteers to run the children's work.

Each year when we report at the Annual General Meeting, or in our Annual Report, we can chart our growth and see how far we have come. We also regularly review where we think we are going.

INVEST YOUR ENERGY IN THE VISION

Once we knew the direction in which we were going, we had to stay focused on what our vision and our values were. It was necessary to clarify our message, and in everything we did we needed continually to ask ourselves: 'Does this fit in with the aims and objectives of the vision that God has for us?

At one time a member of our staff, Emmy, was getting confused about what commitments to take on in her role, as churches were inviting her to speak on many different topics. For me it was simple, because I

'DOES THIS FIT IN WITH THE AIMS AND OBJECTIVES OF THE VISION THAT GOD HAS FOR US?'

used to say to her, 'What are we trying to do? Where are we trying to get to?' Her role, at the time, was heading up the prison work, which we were very keen to see grow. I encouraged her to ask herself: 'Does that task move the vision forward or not? Does it distract you?' Of course, sometimes the Spirit will speak to us and release us, and we have to be free to respond to that. But, on the whole, following the vision is the first priority.

So we would undertake a project only if it would move the vision forward. We have had many opportunities over the years to participate in other areas, but we have had to stay focused on what we believe is our specific calling.

SHARE THE VISION

In order for the vision to take root, it had to be shared with key people in the church, and the congregation as a whole. I remember, in my first week on staff, I received a difficult phone call from the accounts department about how much the development of Alpha outside HTB was costing the church. I remember being really shocked, and saying to Sandy and Nicky, 'You know, I'm not sure whether everybody shares the same vision as you do. If this is what God is doing, I'm not sure that everybody, both on the staff and in the congregation, is on the same page we're on; I'm not sure everyone is actually aware of what God is doing.' We didn't sit down and think through every possible channel of communication to impart and reinforce the message, but I did notice that Sandy, as the church leader, started speaking about Alpha and his vision for the church all the time.

He was leading from the front and using every opportunity – the Parochial Church Council

'... THE MORE PEOPLE UNDERSTOOD AND FELT PART OF THE VISION, THE MORE ENTHUSIASTIC AND COMMITTED THEY BECAME.'

(PCC), sermons, everything he did – to talk about what he felt God was doing. As Ric will outline at the end of the book, the more people understood and felt part of the vision, the more enthusiastic and committed they became.

It is important to recognise that you do not have to do it all on your own – even if you appear to be alone in your church. In our situation, Sandy Millar identified those in the congregation and among the church leadership who were also longing for growth and change. As a leader, you need to identify key people and put them around you – as staff, leaders, or other people in the congregation – to help you realise your vision.

We have needed to build up a team both within the church, and also from outside – a network of other, like-minded churches. At our conferences we encourage people to come as part of a team, and we ensure there is time during the conference for churches from the same geographical area to meet up and get to know one another. This allows friendships and mutual support to develop.

It is really helpful, when you are struggling, to be able to talk to someone who understands your situation and is working towards similar goals. Similarly, you can be a great encouragement to others. All the leaders of HTB church plants get together three or four times a year to meet and encourage one another.

No church's vision, however well thought through, will be realised without the commitment of the community who can make it happen. As Sandy used to say:

> Put the sign on the bus. What I simply mean is tell people as soon you can where you are going. Then they don't have to speculate. If you go out into the high street you will see a number of buses. They have numbers and stops. You can decide whether to get on. As soon as I could I said to them here at HTB, 'We are moving in the direction of the New Testament Church. It'll take time; we might go to Birmingham via Calcutta and Sydney, LA and Brighton, but it's to Birmingham that we are going, that is the direction.'

One church leader tells of how he lost a church plant because he did not repeat the vision enough to people he thought knew it already. In the end they left, and the plant died. Tell people where you are going. Expect to repeat yourself over and over again as you communicate your plans and priorities.

What follows is a structure that might help you to think through how to communicate your vision.

DOCUMENTING YOUR VISION

There are a variety of tools that help to keep us on course and to communicate the vision effectively. These will form the basis for all your communication, whether written or verbal. They include, for example, the following:

The vision statement

This is a brief statement, only a few sentences long, that summarises who you are and what you are hoping to achieve by carrying out the mission of your church. As mentioned earlier, the vision statement of HTB is 'the re-evangelisation of the nations and the transformation of society'.

The five-year plan

The five-year plan is the main vision document. It gives a long-range view of where the church is heading, and where it will be within five years. John Wimber used to say: 'Most

'MOST CLERGY OVERESTIMATE WHAT CAN BE ACHIEVED IN ONE YEAR AND UNDERESTIMATE WHAT CAN BE ACHIEVED IN FIVE.'

– John Wimber

clergy overestimate what can be achieved in one year, and underestimate what can be achieved in five.'

The one-year plan

This is the action plan for the coming year, and the budget flows out of this document.

Quantifying the goals

Quantifying the goals within these action plans enables us to be more specific when communicating the vision. It helps to form images in the minds of people. For example, how many small groups would we like to see on Alpha? How many children attend our children's groups on a Sunday? How many Alpha training events are needed to meet the needs of x number of courses starting?

Who needs to experience the vision?

Once you have formulated and documented the vision, there are a number of different groups that need to hear about it. For example, at HTB we would communicate with the:

- Church committee – (eg the Parish Church Council)
- Leaders (pastorate leaders, worship leaders, Alpha leaders, children and youth leaders, etc)

- Staff
- Congregation
- Broader church community

Defining these groups is a key part in ensuring that the vision is shared appropriately. How you cast the vision and to what depth depends on the grouping. The more key the grouping (eg your leadership groups, the PCC) the more depth and information they need to help them 'own' the vision and impart it, in turn, to the wider community.

WHAT ARE THE BEST WAYS TO COMMUNICATE TO THE DIFFERENT GROUPINGS WITHIN YOUR CHURCH?

For each grouping, decide on the best means of communication. When we introduce a new service on a Sunday, we discuss this fully with the PCC so that we can explain the plans and take questions straight away. When we are encouraging everyone to go to Focus (our annual summer holiday as a church family), we gear up to the main event for months in advance and regularly promote it to the congregation through a variety of ways: via HTB News (a video update of the week's news); our website; email invitations and via social media such as twitter and facebook.

We have found that identifying and developing communication skills is central to making sure that more people understand, and therefore take on, the vision. Where expertise exists in writing or speaking within your congregation, use it to help you communicate the message. Similarly, where someone has a skill in photography, web design or desktop publishing, do not be afraid to ask for help.

'… IDENTIFYING AND DEVELOPING COMMUNICATION SKILLS IS CENTRAL TO MAKING SURE THAT MORE PEOPLE UNDERSTAND, AND THEREFORE TAKE ON, THE VISION.'

Some examples of how we communicate with different groups are discussed below.

Church leadership committee (eg PCC or eldership)

Your church committee meetings are a key time to pray about and build on the vision of the church, and to ensure that all the church's activity is supporting that vision. We meet every other month and begin with supper before the business part of the meeting, as a supportive church committee will be based on good relationships made during this informal time. We have also formed an Exec group, from a number of the PCC who will look at some areas in more depth and who meet on alternate months to the PCC. At HTB the PCC has a 'Quiet Day' once a year, to set aside all the day-to-day business of the church and discuss and pray about the vision God has given them.

Leaders

Leaders' weekend

At HTB we have held an annual leaders' weekend at a conference centre in the countryside. We invite all the leaders in the church – pastorate leaders, Alpha leaders and so on – to go away for a weekend together. Over the course of the weekend Nicky presents what he believes God is calling the church to, and will then work with the leaders and hear from them what the issues are. When we go away on holiday as a church, this also gives Nicky the opportunity to share the vision with the leaders who are there.

Vicarage suppers

Nicky regularly opens up his home to invite the leaders in the church to come for supper and get to know one another, and to discuss the vision together and the part they may play in it.

External conferences

Nicky will seek to take leaders with him when he attends a conference or meeting that he feels might influence the direction of the church. In this way it is not only Nicky who comes back keen to bring about new ideas or changes, but a whole group that understands the values, reasons and models he is hoping to implement. In addition, relationships are built up by attending the same event. When they return, there are more people able to spread the message.

Staff

Staff Day

We have a 'Staff Day' once a year, during which we talk about the direction the church is taking, and what that will mean for the staff. We also enjoy a leisurely lunch, and have time to pray for one another.

Staff prayer meetings

We hold a full staff meeting once a week (see p. 74 for more detail). Each meeting is dedicated to worshipping God, restating the vision, and giving feedback on how we are seeing God fulfil that vision week by week.

Congregation

Restating the vision to your congregation is essential – they need to own it. Repetition is key. You can do this in many ways.

Vision Sunday

We have two 'Vision Sundays' each year, on the Sundays before Gift Days, in September and March. In the sermon we explicitly set out the vision of the church, and what support it will require from the congregation. In preparation for this talk for the congregation, Nicky will share it first with the PCC, pastors and staff to get their thoughts and buy in before Vision Sunday.

Annual review

To coincide with the first Vision Sunday of the year, we produce our annual review. This document includes reports from all the church ministries (and a good number of photographs) explaining what has been going on in the past year, as well as showing the congregation how all resources have been allocated. We distribute a copy to every member of the congregation during the Sunday services.

In addition, the annual look-back DVD is played at every service on our Vision Sundays, the

APCM, and the video is also available to view on our website.

Other Sunday sermons

We regularly take the opportunity on a Sunday to explain how the Bible passage we are teaching on relates to our vision. We give examples of how we see the vision being fulfilled. We talk about Alpha and the related ministries a lot, and have testimonies and stories of the ways God is at work. These are a powerful way of re-illuminating the vision for the congregation.

Website

Our website clearly expresses the vision of the church, both explicitly, by stating the vision statement, and implicitly, by describing all the activities the church is involved with.

HTB News

Every Sunday we show a short video of what is happening in the next few weeks at HTB. Our vision is restated through the activities that happen week by week in the church. This also goes on our web page.

Church weekend/holiday

Every summer HTB hosts a week's teaching holiday, called 'Focus', for the congregation at a holiday camp on the coast. This is an important time for refreshing, re-focusing, and building relationships within the church. It is also an important time in restating the vision of the church and, if necessary, changing direction. While we have found a week to be an advantageous length of time, many of our church plants hold great weekend events, and many of them also join us in this week.

AGM or APCM

In the Anglican Communion every church holds an annual meeting known as the Annual Parochial Church Meeting (APCM). This is where the PCC is elected and we review the previous year's activity and outline the vision for the future. The HTB congregation is encouraged to attend this meeting, to ask questions about the vision of the church and to take part in electing representatives. If an annual meeting is not a standard feature of your church, we would encourage you to consider it, as a year is a good timeframe for marking progress.

Broader church community

No doubt you are involved with ecumenical groups and secular community groups, and you will want to keep them informed of your church's vision.

REFINING THE VISION

Any vision is dynamic. It moves and grows with the organisation and it is important for the vision to be reviewed regularly, and to make sure that its communications are consistent with that vision. How does today's work – a year down the line – compared with the baseline you established when you started the whole process with your parish review? How have you moved on?

> 'ANY VISION IS DYNAMIC. IT MOVES AND GROWS WITH THE ORGANISATION...'

Be prepared to change as you go

At HTB we have often struggled because everything outgrew the structures we put in place. So we have had to create a new structure. I have been at HTB for nineteen years and I think in that time we have probably restructured three or four times. Each time we have gone back to the drawing board, armed with new knowledge and new ideas on our direction, and asked the question – 'How do we make sense of where we are currently, and what do we need to change to get to where we want to be?' In 2005 we went through a key change, as Sandy handed over responsibility for HTB to Nicky. This gave us the opportunity to re-examine and re-align our structures to support Nicky's leadership. More recently, we have instigated a new project complete with a restructure to look at ways to innovate and evolve Alpha, focusing on all aspects of the course and organisation, from resources to training to social media. As we continue to look at ways to best reach the next generation for Christ, we realised we needed to put more energy and resource into the Alpha product and brand. The church cannot afford to have a static organisation.

I have been asked a few times to help other churches review their own structures, and have included three organisational review documents in the appendices of this book. All three are urban churches, but the principles can be applied in any context.

A particular challenge in restructuring lies in knowing when it is right to take the risk of moving on from working strictly with volunteers to having a full-time member of staff. This is an enormous step. At HTB, Alpha had grown to 120 people three times a year before we took on paid staff to support it.

PRAY INTO THE VISION

Everything we do is based upon prayer. We pray that the activities we do are consistent with the vision that God has in mind for us. We pray that God will refine our vision, and will help us to discern it. We pray constantly, and sometimes we find we are in a position where that is all that we can do. Without prayer the vision will never flourish.

TOP TIP: TAKE RISKS

The turtle only advances with its head out of its shell. Be prepared to:

- Take risks
- Use common sense
- Change if it isn't right

2

BUILDING
THE DREAM TEAM

This chapter is all about getting the right people on board. As the body of Christ, every member of every church congregation has a part to play in the fulfilment of that church's vision. Most people are longing to be involved. Their participation enables them to assume ownership of the church's ministries. With the participation of the whole congregation, a church can afford a big vision.

'MOST PEOPLE ARE LONGING TO BE INVOLVED. THEIR PARTICIPATION ENABLES THEM TO ASSUME OWNERSHIP OF THE CHURCH'S MINISTRIES.'

We have always relied on volunteer support from the congregation to enable every ministry in the church to operate effectively. This voluntary support continues today, even though we have more staff than many churches.

From the children's work to the worship team, to Alpha at HTB itself, we enjoy the dedication and commitment of our congregation. In many ways the staff sees its role as enabling the participation of the congregation in God's vision for the church.

Nicky spends a lot of time suggesting ways each person can play a part, and every job is significant – even if it seems minor from a secular point of view. He encourages everyone to express what is their passion, and he wants to release them and support them in pursuing it. For example, Nicky asked a long-standing member of the congregation what her passion was, and she said 'reducing the burden of debt'. Nicky encouraged her to establish a debt counselling service for the church, which was launched and is still running, successfully, to this day.

Another member who joined the church through Alpha was running his own very successful business but had a passion for raising funds. Nicky asked him to head up the fundraising that we needed to do each year for HTB and Alpha.

Recruitment is of the highest priority. If you get the right people they will transform what you are trying to do. The right people in leadership roles will also pick a good team to work with: if you have the right person heading up the children's work they will be able to recruit the best helpers. Similarly, recruiting the wrong people, whether as staff or volunteers, can create real obstacles. Once the wrong person has been appointed it is often harder to put things right. It is certainly more difficult than leaving a position open, and then patiently waiting for the right person to come along.

People, not technology, make the difference. Tools and products can be seductive because they make life easier, but ultimately it will be the right person who drives a ministry – not equipment or resources. We have found that investing in getting and keeping the right people always pays off.

However, actually getting people involved is not always straightforward. Over the years we have identified effective approaches for getting this done.

✔ TOP TIP: PEOPLE FIRST, THEN DO

When you have a vision that calls for something to be done, put the people in place before you begin. Nothing gets done without the right people.

HAND-PICK THE RIGHT PEOPLE FOR THE RIGHT JOBS – SEARCH VS SELECTION

It is important to take a proactive approach to building your team, rather than simply waiting for them to come to you. Some of our best people have been headhunted and handpicked and we always try to take a long-term view and headhunt for tomorrow, not for today. We try to choose people who will grow with the organisation rather than be left behind as it changes.

'IT IS IMPORTANT TO TAKE A PROACTIVE APPROACH TO BUILDING YOUR TEAM, RATHER THAN SIMPLY WAITING FOR THEM TO COME TO YOU.'

We long for every member of the church to be involved and we want them to be released into what they feel passionate about. We encourage this every Sunday at our services. It is, however, also important that your congregation knows the volunteer needs of the church. Once you have identified the various jobs that need to be done, find ways to promote the options to the congregation. However, for key roles, and particularly leadership roles such as pastorate leaders or Alpha leaders, we do not advertise the need. As mentioned, we go and find them, as we find a more personal approach yields better results.

A key skill required for those in church leadership, at any level, lies in identifying those in the congregation who can help – and asking them for that help. When we know what people's gifts are, we can then match them to a particular role. When we ask for help, people know that we have confidence in their ability to perform the functions. The very act of being asked is an encouragement to them. Furthermore, you should be looking all the time for gifted people who can make a contribution to the vision, even though you may not have a specific role for them yet.

Here are four areas it is important to consider:

Skill

Aim high: find people smarter than you. It has been said that A people hire A* people and B people hire C people. When recruiting, be aware of your own weaknesses. Get people involved who are better than you in the area concerned. You must get people whose skills complement your own and supplement your weaknesses. The danger is that many of us have a tendency to recruit people like ourselves because we are then not threatened by them. This process can be unconscious. A much more fruitful solution is consciously to recruit people who shine in areas in which you do not – it is a strength to acknowledge that you cannot do everything.

Look out for gifts in each member of the congregation. Encourage people to identify and develop them, and invite them to participate in the activities for which you think they have a leaning. For example, encourage those with gifts of leadership to train for pastorate leadership, and urge the artistic to take responsibility for the aesthetic expression of the church. Inspire people with musical talents to develop skills in worship, and ask technical experts to provide IT support for the church. People appreciate being picked out and chosen for a role. Invite them to take part rather than passively waiting for them to ask to be involved. This is what I mean:

A few years ago, there was a girl called Jamie in our congregation who absolutely loved the vision of Alpha. She just turned up one day and said, 'I want to help.' To begin with she had the mundane job of database entry (we had so many people calling about Alpha that we needed to build a database), and for days she ploughed on doing just that.

It was only when somebody asked me if I knew about her background that I bothered to find out.

I discovered that Jamie had been a management consultant for an international firm, and had been responsible for installing complex computer systems for multinational companies. She had an MBA from one of the best business schools in the world – and there she was at HTB punching data into the computer.

The moment I found out, I knew she was someone we had to move to another role. There wasn't a specific job for her, but she and I worked together to carve out a remit that suited her skills. In fact she went on to become my right-hand person in those early days of the explosion of Alpha, because she had all the skills I did not have. She designed and put in place the entire infrastructure that we would need in the church to be prepared for the growth of Alpha. I knew what we needed to do but I did not know how to do it. She was absolutely the right person for the task.

Relationship

Good inter-staff relations are so important. We have worked hard to establish strong working relationships and friendships within the staff team, and particularly within the leadership. Friendship and chemistry within the leadership team of the church has proved to be a driving force in the vision of HTB. It was essential for me to like and get on with Jamie for her to function well as my right-hand person. We enjoyed spending time together and working together, and it made the job that much more enjoyable and satisfying. Nicky has a strategy group around him, and it is important that he gets on well with them and enjoys spending time with them, as this is a key group that meets three hours per week to implement the vision. Visitors to HTB have remarked on the level of real and meaningful friendship amongst the staff and volunteers.

Organisational fit

A central lesson for us has been to make sure that the people we have brought into the heart of the organisation have shared the values and culture we have sought to establish within the church. Will they represent you well? Will they answer the phone appropriately? Will they handle conflict with grace?

Humility

In our experience, those people who offer their gifts humbly are those who are really ready and willing to serve. We have learned to be wary of those who put themselves forward too enthusiastically because they might have their own agenda in mind, and might not be properly focused on the vision. Christian character is the primary qualification for leadership roles.

In making a decision, I often find it helpful to refer to the three Cs that Bill Hybels talks about when finding people to join the team. Competence, character and chemistry. Can they do the job, are they people of integrity and would I enjoy working with them?

✔ TOP TIP: INTERVIEW WELL

This is very difficult so don't just rely upon yourself to interview – use others, so you have the benefit of another person's experience.

INVESTING IN THE TEAM

Brief thoroughly

Whether you are working with volunteers or employing paid staff, it is essential that the expectations concerning the role – from both sides – are clearly expressed, and mutually understood, before you appoint someone.

Before a person agrees to take on a role in the church, it is a good idea to give them this sort of breakdown:

- An idea of the overall vision of the church and the project they will be involved with, and how their role fits into it. Full commitment is essential
- The general objectives of the role and its specific responsibilities
- A job brief (whether volunteer or paid staff), including:
  - **Specific timing** of meetings they will be required to attend
  - **The frequency** of meetings. Other commitments that come with the role
  - **An explanation** of how much preparation time you believe this role would take
  - **An understanding** of how long you would like the role to last. For example, Alpha leaders commit for thirteen weeks, to cover the course, the training, the weekend, and the celebration
  - **The name of the person** to whom they will be responsible. It is also helpful to identify those they should approach for guidance and support
  - **The extent of their responsibility**, and the boundaries within which they will work
  - **Clarity** on what expenses will be reimbursed

This process is essential to avoid misunderstandings.

Once people accept roles, whether as staff members or volunteers, it is vital that they are then given further information before they start. Once they have had time to review the job brief, we schedule a meeting to:

- Review the parameters of the role
- Introduce them properly to the person they will be responsible to
- Meet other people working on the project so that they get the whole picture, and understand where their roles fit in with others

When we run an event at HTB, many members of the congregation are involved in a whole range of activities, from meeting and entertaining guests, to welcoming people as they arrive. There are also coordinating roles such as heading up the team serving tea and coffee, and overseeing the stewards. Each role has its own job brief, and we talk it through with those people so that they understand exactly what their role is, what they need to do, and when.

Though we choose leadership positions carefully, we allow leaders to choose their own teams, so that they take responsibility for the people around them. We tell them: 'Build up your own team. You select the people who are going to do the work.' And so we grant ownership and responsibility within the parameters of roles.

TOP TIP: SPREAD THE MESSAGE OF QUALITY

Seek excellence in everything you attempt. Always run an event or a project to the highest possible standards. Pay great attention to detail.

Train, envision and empower your team

It is essential to keep investing in your team and to provide good ongoing training to get the best out of them. We find a mixture of theoretical and practical on-the-job training works well. We have found most people learn best and catch the vision through being involved and learning by osmosis.

Keep sharing the vision and big picture with your team. We all know vision leaks so you have to keep reminding them of where they are going and the essential part they are playing.

Resist micromanaging your team. Set the vision and be there to support them but give them the authority and responsibility to do what you have asked them to do. Set the expectations high and establish a culture of meritocracy.

✅ **TOP TIP: FOSTER TEAMWORK AND OWNERSHIP**

Instead of having individuals doing their own thing in isolation, enable a sense of togetherness. As far as possible, work in teams. Value every contribution. Where have we got to? What needs to be done next? What part do we play in it all?

PLACE VALUE ON MANAGEMENT AND ADMINISTRATION

Good administration is absolutely key to the realisation of your vision. I was once chatting to a curate who was running Alpha in the morning and evening. The evening course had over a hundred guests, and I asked what sort of structure they had to help with a programme of that size. That church did not allow any of the clergy to have administrative support. To me it seemed crazy that a pastor's time should be taken up doing all the administration behind a large course.

It is essential to get good administrative support and back-up behind what you are doing. You might be able to do mailing and hand-outs yourself, but perhaps that time would be better spent preparing a talk or doing pre-marriage counselling. That would especially apply if there is someone in your church with administrative gifts, longing to play a part in the vision of your church.

We have needed to learn to identify people with administrative gifts. These are not necessarily people with a great deal of secretarial experience, but they have the attitude and skills of an administrator. We look for people who are 'can-do' people; who say things like 'leave that with me' and get the job done without fuss; who simplify rather than complicate processes.

> 'WE LOOK FOR PEOPLE WHO ARE "CAN-DO" PEOPLE; WHO SAY THINGS LIKE "LEAVE THAT WITH ME".'

Having the right administrator can transform your working life, and it is important that leadership committees ensure that the clergy are properly supported in this way.

In the early days of Alpha, I had a PA who revolutionised my working life. She asked me, 'What is your biggest frustration?' I replied that it was my tending to be in meetings from 9 am until 6.30 pm, and never seeming to have enough time to put into effect what I was supposed to be doing. I am sure you will all know what that feels like. I could not concentrate on meetings because I knew my work was piling up – and so were all the action points from previous meetings.

She just replied, 'Well, not to worry, I'll come in early every morning and we'll "offload" all the action points from the day before. Then I can get started with the work.' I was then free to do everything else I should have been doing.

That sounds simple, but really it's simple only to someone with that particular gift. To have the right person, who understood my way of working and wanted to support me, made all the difference.

Avoid burnout: How to share the load

In most church communities, 20 per cent of the congregation does 80 per cent of the work. This is true of many organisations. Identifying this 20 per cent is a key challenge for any leader.

Once someone is identified as a keen volunteer or staff member and proves to be a valuable asset to the church team,

'IN MOST CHURCH COMMUNITIES, 20 PER CENT OF THE CONGREGATION DOES 80 PER CENT OF THE WORK.'

beware of falling into the over-use trap. Remember that people get burnout. It is so important that, when you find somebody exceptionally good, you do not overburden them by increasingly eating into their time, energy and commitment. Spread the load and give others the chance to be involved.

It is crucial for church leaders to be aware of their own potential to burn out. The importance of delegation, where appropriate, cannot be over-emphasised. At one stage in the growth of Alpha and HTB I was heavily burdened with an awful lot of responsibility. It seemed everybody just kept off-loading work on to me.

Staff would come in on a Friday afternoon with a 'major problem' to solve. In those days my response was: 'Don't worry. Leave it with me and I'll have a look at it.'

So on Friday night I would take home two briefcases of work. I would struggle all weekend trying to solve problems, while the person concerned had a relaxing weekend.

An article a friend sent me from the Harvard Business Review[1] altered all that. The article highlighted the issue of the burdens of employees falling squarely on to the manager's back. I felt it absolutely applied to my current situation. Upon reading it, my strategy changed. Now my response is entirely different. I now reply: 'Well, that is a problem. I'll tell you what, I promise to meet you first thing Monday morning. You go away this weekend and come back with three proposals that might solve it.'

This change in approach has made an enormous difference to the way both I and my team work. Not only has it taken some of the pressure off me, it has reduced the bottleneck that I used to create. This has allowed my team greater responsibility and ownership of their projects, while still enjoying the security of my supervision. Of course the tough part of the process is allowing people to sometimes make mistakes. But as a leader it is imperative that you give space for people to take the initiative and the risk, or you will stifle all that they have to offer.

> '... GIVE SPACE FOR PEOPLE TO TAKE THE INITIATIVE AND THE RISK ...'

✔ TOP TIP: DELEGATE

To work towards your vision successfully, delegation is key. Do not be tempted to think you can do it all – people are keen to help in so many different ways. Release them and release yourself to do only what you can do.

Acknowledge when things aren't working out

Despite any amount of planning or briefing, there will always be times when projects or people simply fail to work. It is inevitable, and it is also inevitable that these situations will be painful. Failure to confront such problems when they occur will benefit neither the individual nor the organisation.

You must face these situations by talking promptly and clearly to the person concerned. In my experience, as long as these issues are resolved with candour and love, people will respond. They appreciate honest feedback. In the end you will also have to communicate with those who have witnessed the problem or been affected by its consequences. I have found this one of the most challenging areas of my role, but keeping the vision in mind has helped me to succeed in these necessary conversations.

✔ TOP TIP: GIVE FEEDBACK

I believe in honest, straightforward feedback. Do not ignore the little things because you are worried about offending somebody. If it is done in love, and for the right motivation, feedback is always a benefit.

Give thanks regularly and appropriately

Make sure you take the time to thank your volunteers carefully, regularly and appropriately. They are the lifeblood of the church. The contribution they make must be recognised and affirmed. At HTB, we hold regular team events and parties throughout the year for all the volunteers who contribute to the life of the church.

We always ensure that at the end of each term those who have helped with Alpha, The Marriage Course, the children's work and so on are properly thanked. This is done both verbally (and this can be as simple as just saying thank you on an individual basis), and by personal letter. We also make a small gift to those who have taken on the job of leadership, or who have shown exceptional commitment.

3

WORKING TOGETHER

When you know and understand your vision, and have identified the key people to help you realise it, you must agree on a plan of action.

How will decisions be made and communicated? How will decisions then be put into effect and followed up? Once issues have been decided, all those involved must know and follow the agreed steps. This will require dedicated commitment on your part. The result will be great satisfaction, as you and your team start to achieve your objectives with efficiency and few misunderstandings.

WHAT, WHEN AND TO WHOM

When I first arrived at HTB, few routine processes were in place. I set about considering how I could give people the authority to make decisions at the appropriate level. I knew that, if I got it right, I would be free to consider the broader strategic issues, and work on those things within my own area of expertise. We looked closely at all concerned. What meetings did they attend? To whom did they report daily? As mentioned in the previous chapter, it is essential for all involved to know their specific responsibilities, so that they can get on with the job. They also need to understand how they fit into the big picture. Without this knowledge they will not get answers to issues outside their areas of direct responsibility.

While we encourage people to communicate directly as much as possible, we have found that a routine schedule of meetings gives people the consistent opportunity to talk things through and make decisions. We have a number of different meetings at HTB. First of all, we have the PCC, which is our elected body of church leaders. You probably have a similar thing. It may or may not be functioning as you would like.

Sandy shared at many conferences how he worked to raise the sights of the PCC, and redefine how it worked. He spoke about how challenging it was to transform that body from a group concerned with such things as redecorating the lavatories, to one that could discuss weightier matters of vision. Nicky continues to keep the PCC focused on the key issues facing the church, and it is always consulted when there is an issue that has major financial implications or which represents a major change in the vision. Every time it meets, the PCC is updated on all-important aspects of the church. The day-to-day running of the church is delegated to a senior group of staff members who meet weekly.

When we were a smaller church, it was easier to make sure everybody understood the vision – where we were all going and the part we all played. It was easier to ensure the values were disseminated to the groups working to pull it all together. As we have grown, we have had to implement a departmental or team structure, so that information can be communicated and discussed with smaller groups.

Each department or area of church life is encouraged to have a weekly team meeting, to encourage the departments to communicate about their different projects. Particular projects will also have specific meetings with people from different departments. Once the vision and strategy have been agreed, the projects can be managed without intervention so long as staff know the boundaries.

HOW

We must make the best use of everyone's time. People often make the mistake of calling a meeting for the sake of it. The purpose of a meeting is to make and implement decisions, generate ideas, reach a consensus of opinion, or move a project or an idea forward to the next stage.

An effective meeting requires some basic work beforehand. Check that the necessary people can attend. Send out an agenda in advance with the relevant documents. This will enable people to know what to expect and will help them prepare. Ask the relevant people to speak on items that are their responsibility.

At the meeting, make sure that an action plan is established. Everyone should leave knowing which actions are their responsibility and when they are expected to have completed them.

You must establish the date of the next meeting. Circulate the minutes immediately so that everybody knows exactly what is expected, and remember to bring your diary to every meeting so you can plan the next one in.

At HTB, meetings are an essential function for organising events and projects. It therefore goes without saying that the right people must be present and that meetings are run effectively, with carefully planned agendas and accurate minutes and action points. These action points should be reviewed at the beginning of the next meeting.

I remember being at two meetings where I noticed nobody was taking any minutes. I should have picked up on it on both occasions. When topics become complicated and there are no minutes to fall back on, you can easily forget what was agreed and who was supposed to be doing what.

From the very beginning, I always documented everything that I needed to act upon in my 'Red Book' – an A4 hardbound book of lined paper. In any meeting, if I have to implement a proposed action on anything, or if anything needs to be done, I always log it as we go along. I have a good memory and juggle lots of things, but no one can remember everything that is agreed in a meeting.

Gradually we introduced the habit of all attendees bringing a notebook and diary to each meeting. We could then note key actions and decisions and agree times for future meetings or events then and there.

While our meetings continue to become more productive, it is an ongoing discipline to remind people of what makes an effective meeting. I believe the more time you spend preparing for a meeting, the better it will be.

My personal strategy at a meeting is to state its purpose, or ask the person in the chair to state it for all. Everybody attends a meeting with personal expectations or understanding, so it is refreshing when the purpose of the meeting is made plain for everyone. Then you can continually return to that stated purpose and stay on track.

John was a curate at HTB. He later started a new church plant in London. When I asked him about his experience of working at HTB, this is what he said:

> One of the things that struck me most on coming to HTB was both the strategic and fruitful way in which meetings were used. There is also something of a vision-generating and vision-perpetuating feel to them. Meetings never just happen for the sake of having a meeting.

✔ TOP TIP: RED BOOK

This is one of my essential pieces of kit – basically a notebook with lined paper, or, of course, a smart device! Our memories can only see us so far – the 'Red Book' does the rest.

OTHER MEETINGS

Once a week, Nicky hosts a senior staff meeting. This is with all those on the staff who are responsible for a key area in the life of the church. All areas of the church ministry are represented: clergy, operations, finance, courses, prayer, worship and so on. This is not an administration meeting. This is a vision and a prayer and a bigger-picture meeting. We make time to have lunch together. If anyone is worried about something, this gives us an opportunity to pray and talk about it. This meeting is not concerned with the detail of things, but rather with the bigger picture of what is happening, and what we should be looking at and doing.

We also have a prayer meeting for all the full-time staff once a week. For that meeting we discourage absence. Of course, if we are on annual leave that is different, but generally we like all the staff to be together on that day. We are a community first and foremost, and we have to come together once a week to support and encourage one another. We have an hour together and we worship, followed by a thought for the day each week by a different member of staff. We then have a short time of feedback on all the excitements that have

'WE ARE A COMMUNITY FIRST AND FOREMOST'.

happened during the past week, and then we pray to thank God for what has happened and to pray about what is going to happen in the next week.

The feedback from the previous week is really key as it allows everyone to feel involved and excited by the vision. We really appreciate when people share stories at this meeting of how God is changing people's lives, especially if we have been stuck behind a desk all week.

The people doing a lot of work behind the scenes are as involved as those doing the upfront ministry. Tuesday is almost like a Sunday service for the staff.

A NOTE ON PASTORAL CARE AND MEETINGS

When I first arrived at HTB, I would often see members of staff praying for one another in meetings. Of course it is vital for all of us to be regularly prayed for and to receive all that God has for us, but what would start off as a meeting about how to plan a Parish Day would often turn into something altogether different and this was frustrating our progress. We have now established a clear distinction between our pastoral and administration time. If a pastoral issue emerges, we will arrange another time to meet to pray about it. We also make sure there are plenty of opportunities for personal prayer – either in staff meetings or prayer meetings. Many of our teams hold a weekly prayer meeting to pray into all the different projects and things they are working on as well, to pray for one another, which continues to build friendship and trust within the teams.

4

MANAGING
NEW INITIATIVES

New initiatives always arise out of a growing
vision, and managing them well is essential to
ensuring that the work you undertake is carried out
efficiently and effectively. All large-scale projects
will always be presented to the church council for
approval before we undertake them, or to the Alpha
International board for Alpha-related activity.

As we have grown, we have had to implement
new systems and facilities. In my time at HTB
we have instigated several major projects. One of
our most important and difficult projects was to
create a single database of congregation names and
addresses. Other initiatives we have undertaken
include projects as diverse as putting a first floor
into our church hall, creating Alpha and HTB

websites, introducing a new café area as part of the bookshop and creating evangelistic Christmas carol services. We have also launched Alpha Live, where all the Alpha talks are put online, introduced a weekly shelter for the homeless, extended our office space, and created a single, automated diary of all church activities. The list is endless and each project seems to require a different set of skills.

When we start a new project, large or small, we have found it essential to have someone on the team who has a good, basic understanding of project management and its principles, as well as personal experience of managing. With project management an awful lot of common sense is involved – although on larger projects we do involve professional architects and IT people. For smaller projects, our minimum checklist typically looks like this:

- Project goal or objective or product
- Plan
- Start date
- Tasks
- Start and end dates for each
- Defining personal responsibility
- The expected result of the task
- End date
- Estimated cost

We also establish a schedule of project meetings to review progress. We evaluate the activities going on and compare them with the project plan. Are we on target? Are we behind in some ways? Changes in schedule or budget need to be reviewed with the appropriate leaders – for example, the church council. Each project needs time devoted to communicating its purpose to the relevant party and for training. There must also be a plan for the continuing operation and maintenance of the completed project.

Each new initiative should be effectively managed. If not, people will be hesitant to take on new ones. Good project management means resources and enthusiasm are not dissipated. We have found that investing in project management training for staff and volunteers has paid handsome dividends.

✔ TOP TIP: PUT STAKES IN THE GROUND

If you are planning an event such as Alpha, announce your plan as early as possible. Put a metaphorical stake in the ground. Do this whether or not you feel fully prepared for it. Putting down these markers will keep people moving towards a goal. It allows progress to take place.

FOLLOW-UP

For every project you undertake: Plan it. Do it once. Debrief. Write up what you have learned about how to do it. This way, when you do it again the following year, it will be improved based on the document you have pulled together. You then go through the whole process again. It is simply learning from experience.

'FOR EVERY PROJECT YOU UNDERTAKE: PLAN IT. DO IT ONCE. DEBRIEF.'

Reviewing every project or event requires discipline. Most of us complete one project, become desperate to leave it behind, and then embark immediately on the next. But reviewing an event or project, however successful, will be hugely beneficial for future plans.

After every event, we encourage guests to complete a feedback form so we can review how it went. We also ask people to gather stories, testimonies or general anecdotal feedback on how successful the event or project has been – what God has been doing, and the influence it might or might not have had. Some of these stories are included on the Alpha website.

We have a policy of holding a review meeting for the team directly involved in any project. A simple process you might use in a review meeting is to ask three questions:

- What went well?
- What didn't go so well?
- What would we do differently next time?

If you fail to go through this process, you will find yourself reinventing the wheel, and repeating mistakes over and again. This system ensures that you will keep improving. It also allows the people involved in the project to celebrate their success, as well as work through any failures and look at how it could be done better next time. It is important to document how projects were done, and any changes to the next one, so that nothing is lost.

TOP TIP: PLAN, DO, CHECK, REVIEW

This tip might seem obvious but in short it is: 'Learn from experience' – which is something we do not always do.

A NOTE ON TECHNOLOGY

As many new initiatives incorporate the use of technology, I thought it would be appropriate to mention our experience of computer systems. Technology is there to help us and to speed things up. It plays a massive part in our working lives, and we have been able to communicate much more widely and swiftly because of email and the internet.

There are advantages and disadvantages. We never forget that we are in a people business, and you will never get a group to move with you if you stick to email. I never think of Nicky as being a remote leader. He recognises the importance of human interaction alongside electronic communication. He also has a policy of signing all his letters personally. This personal touch echoes Sandy's original vision of making all members of the HTB parish feel as embraced and valued as a guest on Alpha.

We take on new technology only when we think it is going to help us in what we are trying to do. We review the costs and benefits of technology carefully. We also have to be absolutely certain that we have the skills to use and maintain it.

5

KEEPING GOING

I hope the techniques and ideas discussed in this book will help you move and enhance your vision. They have developed from years of work – and we are still working on them! If you take the time to put a few ideas into practice, you will notice a difference. Hopefully this will encourage you to try a few more.

After many years at HTB I remain amazed at the perseverance and dedication of its leaders, staff and congregation. As we have grown and changed, our ministry has brought about fresh challenges that constantly motivate me.

Sometimes we can get so tied up with 'realising the vision' that we lose sight of what it is really all about. At such times we begin to struggle and that is when we risk burning out. Avoiding this has to do with our inner resources, and not the external pressures. There is not much we can do about all the things that come at us: they are part and parcel of doing ministry in the twenty-first century. What we can do, and must try to do, is prioritise making stronger internal resources. I know I need to do four things:

STEP BACK AND TAKE A BROADER VIEW

When you are working daily on seeing a small part of the vision being fulfilled, it is important to step out of the detail and remind yourself of where you have come from and where you are going. Review your progress and see how what you're doing ties in to where you're going. I appreciate that, even though I wish everything could be done yesterday, we are moving forward all the time.

STAY ACTIVELY AT THE CENTRE OF THE VISION

For me at HTB this can mean choosing to help on Alpha and actually seeing God change lives. It also means listening to the congregation, who are growing in their ministries. I am fortunate that Nicky takes so many opportunities to address the vision anew.

HAVE FUN!

I like to ensure it is not all hard work and that we have fun along the way. I encourage lots of laughter in the office and friendship on the team.

STAY FOCUSED ON MY OWN JOURNEY OF FAITH

Most importantly, my personal prayer group – as well as the many opportunities to pray with fellow staff and congregation – helps me enormously, and keeps me focused on where I should be. Without all this, and without the ongoing work of the Spirit in my life, it would be impossible for me to fulfil this role.

Working for a church is more than a job; it is a vocation and a passion. We need the active involvement of the Spirit and the support of the church community if we are to succeed. We are a family and a community first.

'WORKING FOR A CHURCH IS … A VOCATION AND A PASSION. WE NEED THE ACTIVE INVOLVEMENT OF THE SPIRIT AND THE SUPPORT OF THE CHURCH COMMUNITY IF WE ARE TO SUCCEED.'

TRICIA'S
TOP TEN TIPS

While we were putting this book together, a few people put forward observations of what made HTB effective in pursuing its vision. They were small, practical, and sometimes seemingly insignificant ideas. You will have come across some of these earlier in the book, and I list them here hoping that they might be of some use. In any event, I would certainly encourage you to look at your own working practices and share them with your team, so you can all work together effectively.

Have a 'Red Book'

This is one of my essential pieces of kit – basically a notebook with lined paper, or, of course, a smart device! Our memories can only see us so far – the 'Red Book' does the rest.

Delegate

To work towards your vision successfully, delegation is key. Do not be tempted to think you can do it all – people are keen to help in so many different ways. Release them and release yourself to do only what you can do.

People first, then do

When you have a vision that calls for something to be done, put the people in place before you begin. Nothing gets done without the right people.

Interview well

This is very difficult so don't just rely upon yourself to interview – use others, so you have the benefit of another person's experience. Recruit for tomorrow, not for today.

Foster teamwork and ownership

Instead of having individuals doing their own thing in isolation, enable a sense of togetherness. As far as possible, work in teams. Value every contribution. Where have we got to? What needs to be done next? What part do we play in it all?

Take risks

The turtle only advances with its head out of its shell. Be prepared to:

- Take risks
- Use common sense
- Change if it isn't right

Put stakes in the ground

Let me give you an example. If you are planning an event such as Alpha, announce your plan as early as possible. Put a metaphorical stake in the ground. Do this whether or not you feel fully prepared for it. Putting down these markers will keep people moving towards a goal. It allows progress to take place.

Plan, do, check, review

This tip might seem obvious but in short it is: 'Learn from experience' – which is something we do not always do.

Give feedback

I believe in honest, straightforward feedback. Do not ignore the little things because you are worried about offending somebody. If it is done in love, and for the right motivation, feedback is always a benefit.

Spread the message of quality

Seek excellence in everything you attempt. Always run an event or a project to the highest possible standards. Pay great attention to detail.

FORMING A VISION

BY RIC THORPE

The first edition of *From Vision to Action* was a brilliant book. I bought a copy for each member of our team at St Paul's, Shadwell knowing that, if they got to grips with its contents, our vision would become a reality. But the book begged a question: how do you get your vision in the first place?

In 2005, I planted a church in East London with a team from HTB. Having come from a place where vision was clearly articulated and known well by its members, I knew how important it was to have a clear vision to communicate what God wanted us to do and how we were going to do it. There followed a challenging struggle to work out for myself, and our church, what our vision was going to be and how it could be formed and communicated so that everyone was excited about it and could get behind it.

I realised very quickly that I was not like Bishop Sandy Millar and Nicky Gumbel, who made it look easy! I had spent many hours sitting in their houses, listening to them, asking questions, watching them and the people they gathered around them. However, I came to realise that Sandy and Nicky themselves had wrestled for many years, sometimes under very difficult circumstances, to see the vision emerge and it was not as easy as it looked.

As I think about the hours spent at my desk, with my leadership team, walking on my own, offloading to my wife, Louie, I know that vision-forming is a process that takes time. It is different for everyone. It may start with a flicker of an idea or perhaps a fully formed impression but it takes time to get that picture from inside your head and heart out to those people who are going to make it happen.

What follows includes some of the steps involved in the vision-forming process and I suggest ways in which we can move from the smallest spark of an idea to having a fully-formed vision.

WHAT IS A VISION?

A vision is a picture of what the future might look like. It is a picture that is different from how things are now. It will involve change. It will

require energy. It will be
fuelled by passion. It will
catch the imagination of
people who hear it and
will draw them in to help
achieve it. It will involve

'A VISION IS A PICTURE
OF WHAT THE FUTURE
MIGHT LOOK LIKE.'

sacrifice and hard work. It will include celebration
along the way. It will change the way people think
and see because of what has happened in the
process. If it is implemented, it will change things
forever. Bill Hybels' definition sums it up well:
he describes vision as 'a picture of the future that
produces passion'.

The people of Israel had a vision of a land
flowing with milk and honey. It was this vision that
kept them alive in the midst of huge abuse as slaves
in Egypt for 400 years, and as they wandered the
desert for forty years.

Jesus gave his listeners a vision of the kingdom
of God painted in different parables and acted out
through healings and deliverances. The crowds
followed him to his death as a result. After his
resurrection, he gave his disciples a vision for
making disciples across the whole world, which
many of them followed until their own deaths.

But visions are not limited to the first century;
there are well-known examples of visions in our

own recent past. Martin Luther King, the leader of the African-American Civil Rights movement, said, 'I have a dream that one day this nation will rise up and live out the true meaning of its creed: "We hold these truths to be self-evident, that all men are created equal."'[1]

In the HTB church network, as Tricia has already stated, the vision is to play our part in the re-evangelisation of the nations and the transformation of society. This has driven people like myself to plant churches and to invest our lives in something worth dying for. Visions are what keep us alive. They fuel our ambitions and plans. They are what excite us. Without them we perish.

So how are visions formed? And how do they grow in our hearts and our minds? How do they catch like wildfire and begin to impact people's lives? How can they be articulated in such a way as to lead to reality?

1. THE SPARK THAT STARTS A VISION

It all starts with a spark: visions are created by a spark. The spark is an idea from outside us that sets our imaginations ablaze. To make a fire, you need some fuel and then a spark or flame to set the fuel alight. The vision is the fire that needs a spark to get it going.

I love watching the adventurer Bear Grylls on TV, banging his flint together over a few tufts of tinder to get a fire going. With great skill he soon has a small flame that begins to grow into warming fire as he carefully stokes it with more wood. As a child, I once tried to light a fire with a flint stone. It was hopeless. There were no sparks anywhere in sight and of course nothing happened.

Where does that spark come from?

Prayer and prophecy

One of my roles when I was at HTB was to accompany Sandy when a church plant opportunity came up. I loved those trips and would usually drop everything to join him if I possibly could.

One such occasion was in February 2004, when we went to see a church in Shadwell in East London. The church was a beautiful old building that had fallen on hard times. It had very few members and was facing closure.

What I remember most was the garden, which was filled with greenery and life despite its still being winter. The archdeacon who accompanied us quoted an Isaiah prophecy that mentioned the 'Highway of Holiness' (Isaiah 35:8). The church lies alongside a busy main road called 'The Highway' and, as he said, 'The desert and the parched land will be glad; the wilderness will rejoice and blossom' (Isaiah 35:1), something inside me went, 'Yes! This church could be transformed. We must seize this opportunity!' And I thought, 'This would be an amazing church for someone,' without really thinking it could be me!

Afterwards, as my wife, Louie, and I contemplated whether we were being called to lead the plant to Shadwell, we both felt it wasn't right for us. Despite our saying no, Sandy kept on asking, 'Have you made your decision yet?' So, Louie and I decided to pray more intensively about it. I went on a short trip to the States and we both journalled our prayers and thoughts and what we felt God was saying. When I got back, after five days away, I remember sitting at our dining room table with our journals out in front of us. We had both been drawn to similar verses and had faced and explored some of our fears. As we talked, our eyes filled with tears as we came to the same conclusion, that God was calling us to go.

The picture of a transformed community began to grow in my mind as I read the verses from the prophecy in Isaiah 35. It describes a landscape being transformed and God's glory being revealed. The chapter commissions people to strengthen the weak and encourage the fearful. It reminds us that

God will come to save. Blind eyes will be opened; deaf ears hear; the lame will leap up; the mute shout for joy! The redeemed of the Lord will walk on the Highway and will enter Zion singing with everlasting joy!

Since the Highway is the fourth busiest single carriageway in London, it made for a great picture of something completely new and wonderful, which began to fuel a passion to see it become a reality!

God will use the Scriptures and prayer to spark our hearts and imaginations with the first flames of a vision and, as we pray, and as we listen, the vision that God has for us begins to take shape.

Personal experience

As a vision begins to form, our own life experiences play a part in bringing it colour and shape. Sandy and Nicky had both been successful lawyers at the Bar in London and, during my time at HTB, I found myself regularly reflecting on the way that experience had helped them form the vision at HTB. Just as in a lawyer's

> 'AS A VISION BEGINS TO FORM, OUR OWN LIFE EXPERIENCES PLAY A PART IN BRINGING IT COLOUR AND SHAPE.'

chambers, there is an openness to hearing ideas to make the best plan. Just like lawyer's pupils, there is a welcoming of young people to take responsible roles without feeling threatened.

I was a member of Nicky and Pippa's pastorate when I first joined HTB.[2] They had inherited the youth group when they joined the church and, as the youth grew into adults, they kept meeting in the Gumbels' home once a week. I quickly realised that I had joined a group that was full of energy and life and fun, who were passionate about following Jesus. Where Nicky and Pippa saw people who could take responsibility, they encouraged them up into it. Members of the group were delegated tasks such as the worship, talks, cooking, clearing up, throwing parties, and organising weekends. It was such fun because it felt safe and alive and it felt as if we all had a genuine part to play in shaping where we were going.

What I notice about HTB now, under Nicky and Pippa's leadership, is a church full of young people who have been given a chance to shape the vision and play their part. And that vision is about the transformation of people's lives – a high calling that is worth giving our lives to.

So a vision draws on our own experiences as it begins to form.

Circumstances

An exciting part of the development of a vision is making connections with what has already taken place. There are examples of men and women who have been used by God to see extraordinary and wonderful change take place. Indeed, there are circumstances in your own life that will help to form the vision that God is growing in you.

I love history – especially that of London. The church in Shadwell is known as 'The Church of Sea Captains' because it served the dock community in the seventeenth to nineteenth centuries, and as a result has seventy sea captains buried in the churchyard. My family traces its naval connections back to Nelson and Trafalgar and Louie has inherited a portrait of an ancestor who was a merchant sea captain – it's hanging in our dining room. Discovering the history of the church at Shadwell gave us a wonderful sense of connection and confirmation.

As Louie and I explored the history of Shadwell, and particularly its naval history, it became clear that the vision for this church involved reconnecting with the dock community. Once it was a church reaching out to the shipping community in Shadwell and Wapping; today's community living here were part of London's newly developing

Docklands, with the Canary Wharf Tower as its iconic symbol. This was the community that had to be reached with the gospel in this new generation of the church.

Circumstances, in the way of local history, prominent people, our own backgrounds, all help form the vision.

People

One of the most exciting parts of church is the people God calls us to work alongside him. There are some who will encourage us and fan the flame of the vision. They colour the vision and make it brighter. The spark that has started a flame in us touches them with a similar effect. The flame soon becomes a fire.

'ONE OF THE MOST EXCITING PARTS OF CHURCH IS THE PEOPLE GOD CALLS US TO WORK ALONGSIDE HIM.'

Others push back against some of the ideas that begin to emerge. It may be a dissenting voice or a spanner in the works. But these begin to help shape the vision. They give boundaries to ideas and identify areas that need caution and care. They provide a sense of reality to the wild dreams we might have. But they also provide a reality that this might actually work.

Louie and I were fortunate to find that a couple in our pastorate at HTB, Henrik and Inger, said they would come with us wherever we planted. When we told them it was into London's East End, there wasn't a moment's hesitation (or so it seemed to us) as they said, 'Count us in. We're coming with you.' They encouraged us and prayed with us and for us and they still continue to do so.

The sparks need the right conditions to make a flame and the people whom we listen to to make that happen.

So these are the sparks that begin to shape our vision. They begin to show an outline, a purpose, a desire to see change.

Once the spark of an idea is there, it can be fanned into flame.

2. FANNING THE VISION INTO FLAME

The next stage of a vision being formed is where it begins to take shape. All kinds of images and thoughts begin to bubble up around the initial idea and these need to be considered in a way that helps the vision to grow.

The prophet Habakkuk is told by God to write down his vision:

> Write down the revelation and make it plain
> on tablets so that a herald may run with it.
> For the revelation awaits an appointed time;
> it speaks of the end and will not prove false.
> Though it linger, wait for it; it will certainly
> come and will not delay.

Habakkuk 2:2–3

This seems to be a great example for us to follow. It involves writing down what we know of the vision, and waiting. There is a time for the vision to be shared more publicly but this waiting period gives a chance for us to develop it as necessary.

Write down the revelation

Different people will do this in different ways. Some keep it in their minds and allow time to shape and adjust the vision as they grapple with it day by day. Others find it helpful to write it down in their journal or in a document. If you're really creative, you might draw it.

I began to write down my initial thoughts in my journal. There were key words like 'transformation', 'growth' and 'resourcing' that we felt were at the heart of what God was calling us to do. We wrote down the Scriptures that we kept talking about as we described the mission ahead and, when we were given prophetic pictures, these were added too.

Make it plain

Some people are able to see clearly right from the beginning how the vision can be worked out and what it looks like in detail from every angle. I am not one of those people.

As we were forming the vision at St Paul's Shadwell, I was recommended a book called *Simple Church*, by Thom Rainer and Eric Geiger,[3] which I found very helpful in this area. Rainer and Geiger had conducted research with 800 churches in the US and found that those with simple visions and simple structures grew fastest and were most full of life. Those churches that had complicated visions and structures had ground to a halt in terms of growth and life. My 'take home' from the book was to wrestle with the ideas that I felt God had laid on my heart and try to 'make it plain', in Habakkuk's words. If I could draw it on the back of a napkin in a coffee shop or quickly describe it using my fingers to make the points, then it would be plain enough to understand and to repeat to others.

For a herald to run with it

Once the vision is in a form that is written and simple, it is time for it to get some traction with others. For visionary leaders this is hard not to do.

I am in a network with other church planters and church leaders who are highly expansive and entrepreneurial. I am used to hearing them cast vision whenever they get even the smallest window of opportunity. Sometimes they need to be reined in!

This is more likely to be a challenge if you are not used to telling others what is on your mind and heart. You might have lots of ideas and vision, but you hold it close to your chest. For you, there comes a time when you have to begin to share it with others: it is important to allow others to hear it and comment on it and have opinions about it. This can be scary. But it is absolutely essential to get it out so that it can become a reality! Follow Habakkuk's advice and write it down so that others can see it and 'run with it'.

Awaiting the appointed time

Habakkuk the prophet goes on to say that there will be a gap between the vision being written down and its becoming a reality. This is the waiting time. It is the time between vision and action.

I believe that this is the time for prayer. It is not down time. It is not wasted time. It is not drumming fingers on tables time. It is prayer time. It is a germination time that is necessary before action can take place.

Take the time to pray. Invite others into praying. Allow the sparks of the vision and small flames to ignite your heart and the hearts of that close group of people you have shared it with.

Many visions don't get started because the vision holder gives up in this waiting time. Impatience kicks in and the vision is crushed because it has been shared too early. My friend Greg once told me that the contrary fruit of the spirit of impatience has been the graveyard of many God-given visions. I think he is right. Visions need a fermentation period or germination time before they are really ready.

Don't get stuck in this place, but don't avoid it either. It is the place where the fire begins to catch and strengthen and grow hot!

3. STOKE THE FIRE

Once the fire takes, it's time to start adding fuel. At each stage of adding logs to the fire, you check it is still stable and able to take the extra weight. The fire needs checking to make sure it doesn't lose its power. It may also need a little tweaking from time to time to gain maximum performance from it.

The process of vision-forming is the same. We need to test the vision with people outside our immediate circle. This is the time to talk it through with the core leaders of the church if you haven't done so already. In our setting, that means talking to three leadership groups in the church: the PCC who look after the governance of the church, the paid and voluntary staff who are managing the day-to-day running of the church, and the pastoral leaders who are overseeing the mid-week groups in the church.

These are groups of people who have the responsibility for implementing the vision and, as such, they need to be completely on board with it. They need to understand it. They need to recognise their place in it. They need to believe in it. And communication is of the essence.

As the vision holder, you need to know how strongly formed the vision is at this stage. Is it essential for it to be formed exactly as you have it in your heart and mind? Or is it ready to be adapted by the leaders who will begin to implement it? If it is adaptable, how much can it evolve?

I found it was important at the planting stage to communicate a clear idea of what the church would look like in certain core areas: the services; the tone of the church; the understanding of who was in authority. But I wanted to enable other areas to have flexibility and creativity, so that those who were with us could help to shape other aspects of church life.

> '… IT [IS] IMPORTANT… TO COMMUNICATE A CLEAR IDEA OF WHAT THE CHURCH WOULD LOOK LIKE IN CERTAIN CORE AREAS…'

I spent considerable time talking about the vision – seeing the transformation of Shadwell and East London by the love and power of God – to leaders and to the church on Sundays and midweek. I used conversations with members as opportunities to explain the vision. Conversations are two-way so it gave me the chance to hear how the vision was being received and understood. Inevitably there were adjustments as people and groups had ideas and made comments that enhanced the vision. The best part of it was hearing stories as people applied the vision to their lives – encounters with local people, answers to prayer, seeing new people arrive, and seeing new creative ways of mission emerging.

Encouraging the congregation to get on board

A new vision may mark the end of some things that were very important to some people and it is key to think through the best ways of communicating and encouraging the new vision in a way that helps get everyone on board.

An old friend, Andy, came to help us think through the process of change that was needed to get everybody on board. He used a picture (below) of the sea crossing from one piece of land to another to help us to think through moving towards where God was calling us to be. Our old thinking is the 'the old land' and our new thinking or vision, is the

'the new land'. The picture helped people to locate themselves in the process. It also helped people understand where others were, so that there was greater understanding in the whole process.

The picture can help to show that people experience the process of catching the vision in a number of ways – some are excited (sailing across in a yacht), others are afraid of change (hanging on to a tattered raft). Some see it as fun (dolphins in the water), others as unsafe (the shark and the rocks). This helped me understand that some of my vision-casting needed to address specific issues that helped people to believe in following it.

Second, we realised that we needed to mark the end of some activities and contributions in an appropriate way. We marked the leaving of a couple of leaders with a big send-off party. This enabled us to stop certain activities and meetings overtly. I effectively said, 'These people have made a fantastic contribution. Their going means things will be different. Some things will stop now. We will miss the people and the activities but we need to move on.'

In the same way, we celebrated the beginnings of a more missional approach with a short four-week series called 'Bite-sized vision'. We had a short, 'bite-sized' presentation of the new approach to our vision, each week using a different chocolate bar that we gave out to the church. I love chocolate, so it seemed a good way of sharing my passion with others! We also showed a short video that summarised the different ways the vision was working out in practice, and gave out a card that make it clear in print.

So whether it's chocolate or something else that's fun, it is good to stoke the fire of the vision in different ways to get it burning in people's hearts and minds.

4. TURN UP THE HEAT

The next stage of finding and developing the vision is to help those who are hearing it start thinking about how they fit into it themselves. This phase is where the intensity of the vision begins to grow because the church is turning from listening to the vision to beginning to talk about the vision.

'... HELP THOSE WHO ARE HEARING [THE VISION] START THINKING ABOUT HOW THEY FIT INTO IT THEMSELVES.'

Once I had communicated the vision to the church and begun to develop the detail of the vision with each group of leaders, we invited the leaders to think through what the vision looked like from their point of view.

I took the leaders away for a weekend and we explored five different aspects of the vision: our worship, our discipleship, our mission, our long-term legacy and the behind-the-scenes working of the church, called the engine room (see Chapter 1). We spent time in worship and prayer, reflecting together on what God was saying to us. We then worked out what the overall vision looked like through the lens of these areas of church life. The leaders split up into teams, according to their personal preference, to focus their efforts on each area.

What emerged was a clear statement of the vision for that area of church life and a list of measurable goals for the next two to five years. It was very useful to have this on paper. But far more significant was having the leaders buy into the vision and work out how to apply it themselves.

By the end of the second afternoon, we put all the statements together and came up with a document that effectively said, 'This is what we are about as a church' (see Appendix 2 for further information on St Paul's Shadwell vision). We prayed more and then had a party! What a great way to finish a vision weekend!

The sharing of the vision had moved from top-down communication to a more viral form, as leaders and then members caught the vision. While the vision-catching is becoming viral and the heat of the fire of the vision is increasing, there is still a vital place for the leader to preach the vision. The leader can keep intensifying the heat by re-emphasising the main thrust of the vision again and again through preaching, meetings with leaders and ministry meetings.

5. SPREAD THE FIRE

The last stage of the vision-forming process is to write down the vision in a way that can be published for all to see. This means that new people coming to the church can quickly see what the vision is and catch it for themselves.

'... WRITE DOWN THE VISION IN A WAY THAT CAN BE PUBLISHED FOR ALL TO SEE. '

There are plenty of ways to do this and it is good to use any method you can to make sure it is understandable and accessible to those you want to see it.

After our leaders' weekend, we published our vision document and formally adopted it at our Annual Parochial Church Meeting. We asked the whole church to pray into every area of the vision and kept encouraging them to apply it to their own area of church life as well as adopting it into their own prayers and lives.

After that, we have looked for ways to publish the vision document as broadly as we can. We put it up on a notice board in church for all to see when they arrive at the church. We published it on our website. We have filmed a simple video that articulates the vision online. We have used the vision document publicly in meetings throughout the life of the church. We articulate it when we have our vision days twice a year.

As Tricia has commented earlier in the book, it is essential to keep communicating the vision so that it is affirmed and reaffirmed and so that everyone becomes familiar with it and understands it. The leaders might feel they're doing it too much, because they are repeating it all the time, but it takes a longer time than you think for the vision to be embedded throughout the whole church.

I remember Sandy Millar telling the story of a conversation between him and his wife, Annette, about communicating the vision at HTB. Sandy had been frustrated that people were being slow to pick up what he felt God was doing, saying and encouraging in the church. Annette said to

> 'VISION LEAKS AND IT NEEDS TIME TO SINK IN.'

him, 'They haven't got it.' He said, 'I told them in a sermon last November. I made it really clear.' And Annette said, 'Well, they haven't got it!' Sandy reflected that we might feel we have told people at one time or another, but they don't *get* it unless you keep on telling them, again and again. Vision leaks and it needs time to sink in.

TIME TO TURN YOUR VISION INTO REALITY

This process of forming a vision is challenging and exciting for any leader or group. From getting the sparks of the vision, to fanning it into flame, to stoking the fire, to turning up the heat, to spreading the fire, a vision takes time and energy and prayer.

Once you have your vision, it's then time to turn it into action.

APPENDICES

APPENDIX 1: ORGANISATIONAL REVIEWS

I was invited to spend a day with three very different churches. Following are examples of those specific churches and the structures we recommended, in consultation with their leadership, in order to create a platform for growth.

CHURCH A

Church A is an Anglican church with a congregation of 700.

Organisation and management review

Together with the Head of HR, I spent the day with the church leader and the team at Church A. The purpose of the day was to see if we could assist the church leader with some suggested structures. This summary report details our observations and recommendations.

1. Core team/board
It is important to establish a core team around the church leader. All activities and ministries are to report in to one of the board members.

The board would be the church leader, the assistant minister, the curate, the family life and morning Alpha leader, the pastoral coordinator and the office manager.

2. Meeting structures
Each meeting should have clear aims and objectives, an agenda (timed or at least a time limit on the whole meeting) and be minuted. Suggested meetings:

2.1 Vision and strategy meeting
This would include prayer and would be held once a month or once a term. Attendees would be the board members. There would be no administration at this meeting; instead it would be much more forward-looking.

2.2 Core team meeting, aka board meeting

This would be once a week and would give approval for new projects, expenditure over a certain amount and act as an escalation point for policy-making decisions. This is not a vision meeting.

2.3 Whole staff meeting

This would be once a week and should incorporate a run-through of events coming up during the week.

2.4 One-to-ones

a) The church leader with direct reports

These should be fortnightly. It is an opportunity for each of the core team to review their areas of responsibility with the church leader and to report how they are moving projects and tasks forward.

b) Core team and direct reports

These should be weekly or fortnightly. Similar to above, each manager should review areas of responsibility with people on their teams.

2.5 Services meeting

This should include the church leader, the family life and morning Alpha leader, the assistant minister, the curate, the pastoral coordinator, the children's worker, the youth worker and the worship leader. These should be weekly. The aim is to discuss feedback and actions arising from the previous Sunday and include planning for the next Sunday services.

3. Technical requirements for the office

There is an immediate requirement for the following to be addressed:

- Proper management of incoming telephone calls
- Networking of PCs for sharing information, particularly the database

These areas can be discussed in more detail once the office manager is in place.

4. Working time for support staff

There is a need for continuity of effort in bringing together the requirements for Sundays (in particular) and possibly other events such as Alpha. It is therefore recommended to have support staff responsible for these events present on the day to ensure all goes to plan. Responsibility for smooth running at the event will be with support staff, NOT the pastoral staff, freeing the latter to do the course teaching and look after the guests.

5. Suggested responsibilities

Church leader

Clergy role, and oversees everything but with particular 'hands on' for:

- Prayer
- General Synod
- Special courses
- Accountability of core team

Family life and morning Alpha leader (reports to church leader)

- Family life
- Children
- Morning Alpha
- Parish weekend
- Women's work

Assistant minister (reports to church leader)

- Clergy role
- Alpha
- Mission
- Men's ministry
- Post-Alpha discipleship course
- Pastoring
- Pastoral care support

Pastoral coordinator (reports to church leader)

- Pastorate coordinator
- Home groups
- Prison Alpha
- Publishing, promotions and communications
- Bookshop
- Registration forms
- Link to Home Focus
- Parish magazine

Office manager (reports to church leader)

- IT
- Web
- Finance
- Building project
- General administration and reception
- Facilities management
- Diary
- Database
- Personnel

Curate (reports to church leader)

- Clergy role
- Prison Alpha
- Ministry and leadership training
- Worship team
- Pastor
- Youth

- Special services
- Sunday services
- Newcomers
- Volunteers

6. Challenges

a) New appointments

We think you have a wonderful core team, which is a great blessing and a key foundation on which to build. The appointment of the office manager is a key next step, and the recruitment of quality support staff is key to moving the vision forward.

b) Enlarging the pastoral coordinator's role

In section 5, we have considerably enlarged the pastoral coordinator's areas of responsibility. They (as well as the family life and morning Alpha leader) will need further support staff to carry the workload. At present, we have indicated bookshop as part of the pastoral coordinator's brief. This was because logically it fits with publications and communications but we appreciate there could be issues with this so this can be a discussion item.

c) Team working

Presently, people tend to work independently. There is a need to work more in teams. An example would be:

> The family life and morning Alpha leader is responsible for the parish weekend. Therefore they need to gather together a project team to cover areas such as: children, youth, administration (promotion and registration and volunteer tasks) and worship.
>
> They will also need one of the clergy team to be responsible for the teaching programme at the weekend.

Another example would be the services meeting described in 2.5.

CHURCH B

Church B is an Anglican church with a congregation of 200.

Organisational review

Together with the head of HR, I spent the day with the church leader, the church leader's wife and the team at Church B. The purpose of the day was to see if we could assist the church leader with some suggested structures. This summary report details our observations and recommendations.

The vision

To have three vibrant and dynamic churches forming the Church B District Church Council; to be community based and to have the full involvement of the local people.

In our individual meetings with the team we asked what they regard to be the key priorities. The clearest expression was summarised as Sundays, pastorates, Alpha and community work. That said, not everyone in the team was clear about the priorities, and in this sense it may be beneficial for the church leader to articulate his vision and how the priorities fit into it at a forthcoming staff meeting.

Staff structure

We recommended that the structure be further defined, so as for there to be clear reporting lines, a distinction drawn between pastoral support and line management, and greater accountability for junior staff. In addition to this organisational structure, it is of course anticipated that the church leader and the person responsible for pastoral ministry will continue pastoring the team.

Leadership team

If the above structure is set in place, the leadership team will form as the church leader, the curate, the worship leader, the person responsible for pastoral ministry (ideally female, if not the church leader's wife), and another member of clergy. It may be beneficial for this group to meet together on a fairly regular basis – perhaps weekly to begin with to roll out the vision and strategy.

Curate

We suggested that, in addition to clergy responsibilities, the curate is encouraged to take the lead in defining and implementing the strategy for 1) Alpha and 2) evangelism and community work as defined above in the vision, partnering with the person responsible for pastoral ministry.

Clearly the curate will need support from the team so to implement, but this adjustment in approach is an important one in order for the curate to be able to operate as a senior member of the team, and not, for example, the one shopping for groceries for Alpha on a Wednesday afternoon. We exaggerate to make the point. We believe that giving the curate responsibility for managing two (initially three with the children's worker) pastoral assistants will develop their delegation and leadership skills, and that giving responsibility for the community work will ignite their passion. The curate does not need to be the vision bearer – that will of course come from the church leader – but with a team of pastoral assistants the curate will be better equipped to lead. A mentor could provide valuable support for the curate.

Need for an implementer

The church leader made a comment about things just happening at HTB. Having met with the team, it is evident that no one on the staff shines as a natural implementer – someone to set the operation in motion and make it happen so as to release the clergy and ministry-focused staff. I think we are all agreed that the current key high-capacity volunteer (who has a consultancy/

technology background) would be ideal in this role. They are passionate about the vision and able to volunteer their time. We would recommend that they sit in the core team as a consultant, taking on a special projects role and reporting to the church leader and perhaps occasionally participating in the leadership team meetings.

Pastoral assistants

In the short term we would recommend that the pastoral assistants have their roles defined with a job description, acknowledging that things need to be fluid, especially in a team of this size. Looking to the autumn, if one pastoral assistant is to leave for theological training, it could be that the youth worker steps into this role. This may then best fit reporting in to the additional clergy, allowing the curate to ascertain the exact skill set required for his team – possibly verging, logistics and administration. In time, the pastoral assistants may be required to provide the worship leader and the person responsible for pastoral ministry with administration support – we recommend that this be assigned by the church leader so as to maintain clear reporting lines.

Infrastructure: technology and database

The key high-capacity volunteer is running with this project and appears to have an excellent grasp of the opportunities and challenges.

Church leader's PA

As discussed, the church leader's PA is not attending the Sunday morning service at the church. We recommend that this is addressed. During the week, the church leader's PA is often the face and voice for the church within the parish and it would be of great benefit if they were able to get to know the congregation so to effectively support the church leader and run the office. When the church leader is away at weekends, and if both the church leader and his PA are away in August, there needs to be a solution to access emails and post. Similarly, some of the team mentioned that the PA is sometimes in a vulnerable position when alone in the office and opening the door.

Succession plan

Given that the curate has only committed to Church B for a further year until the end of his curacy, it would be helpful to plan some form of clergy succession strategy.

Communication strategy

Many of the team talked about empowering the congregation to get connected and involved, from being absorbers to transformers. Currently this is happening through the pastorates. The curate's wife or the key high-capacity volunteer would both be great at pulling together a strategy for communication with the congregation.

The curate's wife

The curate's wife will be a great asset to the team, and definitely worth approaching to see if she is able to spearhead something – mother and toddlers for example. People speak very highly of her and we are sure she would love to be involved.

CHURCH C

Church C is a multi-denominational church with a congregation of 600, with a further 350 people attending weekly outreach events.

Organisational review

Together with the head of HR, I met with the church leader and his core team at Church C. The purpose of the day was to see if we could assist the church leader with some suggested structures. This summary report details our observations and recommendations.

The vision

Following a period of explainable disorientation, the last eighteen months have seen a period of consolidation for Church C. The leadership team is new and a strategy has been established. Church C uses a group of twelve or G12 model – a fresh vision of church originating in Colombia. Part of this vision involves structuring and leading the church with two core groups of twelve, who in turn have a faith goal to disciple their own twelve, and equip each individual to do the same thereafter.

Strong core activity exists in 1) caring for the homeless and 2) overseas mission – reflecting on the church and the kingdom, both local and global.

The vision is to position themselves to reach the thousands for Christ, rather than simply adding numbers to the membership total – 'the world is our parish' philosophy.

Recommendations

1. Core team structure
'Put your best people on your biggest opportunities, not your biggest problems.'

It is beneficial that a high proportion of the staff also enjoy membership of the core group of twenty-four.

1.1 Having reviewed the structures, we would like to recommend one of two options to ensure that the church leader is appropriately supported and released to drive the vision forward. Either:

- Bring in a personal assistant for the church leader, under the operations manager or as a church leader direct report (see diagrams A and B)
- Divide the current remit of the operations manager in anticipation of the inevitable administration growth given the end of the recent consolidation phase. Bring in another experienced manager to deliver aspects of this role. The positioning of this role would

need to be handled with sensitivity given the operations manager's current remit, valuable relationship with the church leader and contribution to the church's vision (see diagram C, below)

1.2 In any event, it is clear that the operations manager role requires definition and clarification – so as to match the operations manager remit and skill set.

1.3 Another way of looking at this would be to split the structure into a) ministries and b) operations. Those individuals sitting in a ministry role will inevitably need to report to the church leader. Aside from that, we would recommend that a number two for the church leader (which could be the operations manager) would head up all the infrastructure teams – Finance & IT, Office, General Management and Strategic Planning (see diagram D).

1.4 We discussed at length the fact that the office manager is overstretched and unable to operate at a level that adds most value. It is clear that an effective office administrator is required to release the office manager from day-to-day administrative duties.

2. Priorities

The team is currently looking to move into a new office space. Securing a new location has to be a priority and the church leader requires a project manager to coordinate this activity. This could be the church leader's number two or another church manager who has the relevant project management and implementation skills. In addition to this, we would recommend the formation of a committee of volunteers from within the congregation who have various skills and levels of time to help on a project of this magnitude.

3. Communication

It is evident that strong channels of communication exist within the core team, both within the staff and within the two senior 'twelves'. To further this and to aid transparent, inclusive and timely communication, the following forums are suggested:

3.1 Staff meeting – weekly. The primary aims of such a forum are to provide a fixed point in the week for corporate prayer and worship, and an opportunity to look back and forward with respect to aspects of ministry areas and business.

3.2 Senior 24 meeting – weekly. This is already in place, and given the G12 model is definitely required. We would recommend that points of action and information flow from the staff meeting to the senior 24 meeting and vice versa, to aid a consistent approach.

3.3 Vision and strategy meeting – monthly. Only required if the weekly staff and senior 24 meetings do not provide an opportunity to discuss and brainstorm the medium–long-term picture.

4. Volunteer vision – tapping into talent

We would recommend that, wherever possible, graduates of the church's leadership programme are positively encouraged to get involved and serve as their gifts and skills warrant in a volunteer capacity, in addition to serving within their twelve. Establishing this model from the outset will encourage the use of volunteering in this way and limit the pressure to increase staff headcount. So as to have gravitas, such a vision for volunteering needs to be preached from the top.

5. Working practices

It is evident that all members of the core staff are fully on board with the vision and thoroughly flexible with respect to working hours. While extremely beneficial, this needs to be monitored to ensure that staff do not burn out.

That said, and for the reasons discussed at our meeting, we think that, where staff have responsibility for a particular aspect of ministry or event (eg the administration of Sunday services), they ought to be contracted to work the event. This may result in changes to contractual hours for some staff and the establishment of a time off in lieu policy.

6. Recruitment

'When in doubt, don't hire – keep looking.'

We would recommend that you continue to look for an office administrator and think creatively about how to attract an individual with high levels of motivation and positivity who can be shaped and nurtured by the office manager.

7. Church C calendar of events

Having one of the core team oversee the coordination of the annual calendar of events would ensure that the execution of these projects is planned more proactively and coordinated holistically with the ministry workers still running with the detail. The operations manager or the office manager could fill this role. It is important to set this structure in place now so as to support the inevitable growth in number and type of events going forward and to benefit from efficiency wherever possible.

Diagram A

church leader

operations
manager

pa to church
leader

Diagram B

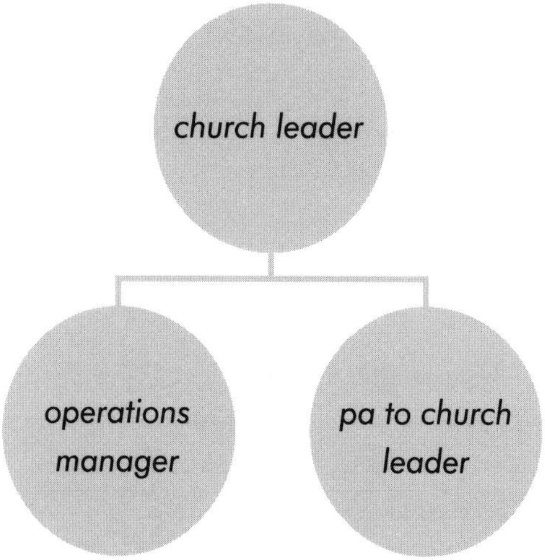

Diagram C

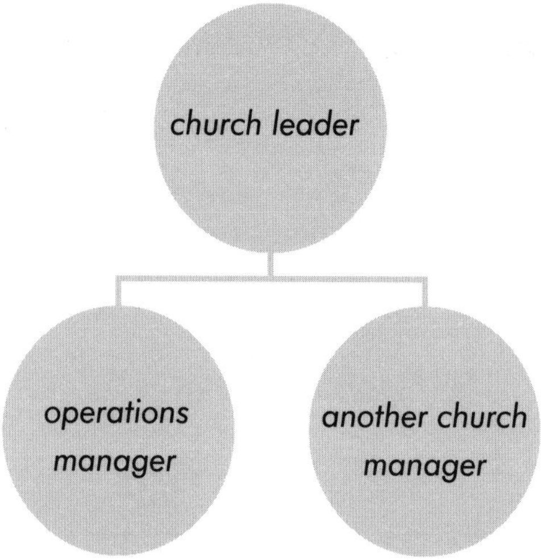

Diagram D

church leader

ministries

operations & management

ministry staff

church leader's no 2

APPENDICES

APPENDIX 2: ST PAUL'S SHADWELL VISION DOCUMENT

ST PAUL'S SHADWELL VISION – 2010 AND BEYOND

1. The vision statement

We want to worship Jesus, build his church, love our neighbours, and transform East London by the love and power of God.

2. The visible vision

A church characterised by: worship of God that is Spirit-inspired, committed and consumes the whole of life; fellowship that is caring, deep and open; outreach that is compassionate and contextual in response to the love of Jesus for us and in order that the kingdom of God may grow.

This can be described in four movements, seen in every area of church life:

Upward: We want to grow in our love of Jesus through excellent Sunday services, connect groups and ministries that offer a warm welcome, passionate worship, relevant Bible teaching, and powerful ministry of the Spirit.

Inward: We want to grow in our love for each other through encouraging everyone to be an active member of a connect group, discipling one another in smaller accountability groups and also helping to build up the church through serving one another.

Outward: We want to grow in our love for our neighbours (in neighbourhoods and networks) through getting to know them, sharing our faith, running Alpha, building a specific missional purpose in each connect group and growing ministries and partnerships relevant to our context.

Forward: We want to see God's kingdom grow across East London (The East End is 25 square miles) over a generation (25 years) through forging partnerships with churches, social enterprises and charities, planting churches, and reinvigorating institutional and civic life (by working with schools, businesses, local government, public services and community organisations).

3. The values of the vision
We want to be a church that is marked by:

Intimacy with Jesus – which leads to an emphasis on worship, prayer, and ministry of the Spirit and on which our relationships are based.

Generosity to others – which seeks the healing and wholeness of people's lives, in which everyone is involved and which resources others by giving away what we have been given by God.

Mission to the world – which looks outwards, engages in evangelism and seizes every opportunity we are given to help God's kingdom grow.

Overall we want to see Jesus' kingdom grow, leaving a lasting legacy in East London, in the cause of which everyone at St Paul's Shadwell can play a part.

NOTES

CHAPTER 2: BUILDING THE DREAM TEAM

1. William Onken Jr. and Donald L. Wass, 'Who's Got the Monkey?', *Harvard Business Review*, November–December, 1974.

FORMING A VISION

1. Martin Luther King, Jr, 'I Have a Dream', delivered 28 August 1963, at the Lincoln Memorial, Washington DC.

2. A pastorate is a smaller grouping in the church where people meet to grow as Christians. For further information, see *Pastorates – Life at the Heart of the Church* (Alpha International), 2006.

3. Thom S. Rainer & Eric Geiger, *Simple Church: Returning to God's Process for Making Disciples* (B&H Publishing Group), 2010.

FURTHER RESOURCES

The From Vision to Action website offers further talks and resources on church growth from the Vision to Action Conference and the HTB Leadership Conference – please go to **www.fromvisiontoaction.org** to find out more.

Below is a selection of publications that you might also find helpful.

ALPHA RESOURCES

Integrating Alpha into the Church DVD
(Available online at alpha.org)
What sort of church are we trying to build? How do we develop a church that is relevant to today's society? In this DVD, the Rt Revd Sandy Millar discusses biblical principles for today's church and practical ways that Alpha can be integrated into the church.

Nicky Gumbel – Questions of Life
(Alpha International, 2010)
The Alpha talks in book form. Containing the fifteen talks, this is essential reading for anyone involved in Alpha.

Nicky Gumbel – Telling Others: How to Run the Alpha Course
(Alpha International, 2011)
This book imparts the vision, excitement and challenge of Alpha and is for churches who wish to run the course within their communities. It includes material from the Alpha conference and provides course administrators and leaders with insight and helpful guidance on the practicalities of Alpha.

WHAT HAPPENS AFTER ALPHA?

Pastorates – Life at the Heart of the Church
(Alpha International, 2006)
Christians have always met together and, from the earliest beginnings of the church, members of the community of faith have gathered in both small and large groups. This guide provides tips on how to integrate Alpha guests into the discipleship life of the church, and includes practical advice for leaders on how to set up 'pastorate' or 'mid-week' groups, including the purpose and place of

pastorates, the practicalities of an evening and the role of a leader.

ALPHA FOLLOW-UP COURSES

Nicky Gumbel – The Jesus Lifestyle
(Alpha International, 2010)

Eighteen Bible studies that seek to apply Jesus' teaching on the Sermon on the Mount to our daily lives. This book shows us how Jesus' teaching flies in the face of the modern lifestyle, and presents us with a radical alternative.

Nicky Gumbel – A Life Worth Living
(Alpha International, 2010)

This nine-session course, based on Paul's letter to the Philippians, is aimed specifically at those starting out in the Christian life and is ideal for those who have just completed Alpha. Each chapter gives practical and positive guidance on how to achieve a new and fulfilled life – a life worth living.

Nicky Gumbel – Searching Issues
(Alpha International, 2013)

Nicky Gumbel tackles the seven most common objections to the Christian faith in this new edition, including suffering, other religions and the New Spirituality.

OTHER USEFUL RESOURCES

Bill Hybels, *Courageous Leadership* (Zondervan, 2010).

Graham Tomlin, *The Provocative Church* (SPCK, 2008).